Modern Garden Design

The Big Book of Ideas

Modern

Text Ulrich Timm   *Photography* Gary Rogers

Garden Design

The Big Book of Ideas

Modern Garden Design

6 *Trends in* **modern** *garden design*

A garden for every lifestyle. From minimalism to relaxing by the pool; architectural planting for structure in the garden; new materials in unexpected contexts. Lighting from a different perspective; tactile art; let's cook dinner in the garden.

34 **Today's** *gardens*

Living for the moment; new ways to enjoy the garden. Dive into the pool and spend a moment in meditation; enjoy the vista, be amazed by the mix of materials, and appreciate the finer details. Relax in ground-breaking new architectural surroundings, or just simply lounge around. What about the gardening? Only the basics are required.

82 **Modern** *components*

The lure of minimalism. Clear structures instead of contrived garden landscapes. New materials such as crushed glass find their niche in the garden and even pebbledash experiences a revival. Glass and steel make a cool combination, and the only color comes from flowers.

Modern Garden Design

124 **Modern** *planting*

Contrast is the name of the game. Dark foliage is as much sought-after as delicate ornamental grasses. The spherical forms of allium and box continue to be popular. Wild flowers and unusual color combinations are the latest additions. Grasses are high, conifers are low and willow is woven.

166 **Modern** *extras*

Amazing eye-catchers which give the garden a new look. It could be a whirlpool, a tall, slim container; mirrors or a fantastical glass orb. What about a moon gate, or fine art made from natural stone? Take a look at the gabions – mesh baskets filled with stone, normally left in the background; ways for a light source to illuminate the night garden.

202 *Appendix*

Trends in **modern** *garden design*

Stone, water and plants

Water is a familiar feature in today's gardens, usually in the form of fountains, streams and rills, fishponds or swimming pools. But water can also promote a sense of calm, or function purely as a reflective surface. Of course, the reflections off the surface of a pool of water can be stunning, but sometimes, we need to go further …

The garden

This section of the garden brings together some of the natural treasures of our planet: stone, water and plants. Although the concept is not without precedent, they have been combined and presented here in a very original way. Stone is present in two forms: limestone fragments and rough-hewn slabs. A marsh bed in the water is completely covered by irregular quartzite tiles, carefully layered, making an interesting and innovative feature. There are two bodies of water: one is a narrow canal, 20 inches (50 cm) wide, formed by the marsh bed; behind it we see a much larger sheet of water. Lastly, there are two types of plants: the juneberry with its multiple branches, as seen here in the foreground, and the vibrant Japanese iris (*Iris ensata*). The long, narrow leaves reach up from the carefully placed quartzite tiles, and their reflections in the still water present a magnificent sight. Not an extravagant display, but beauty, harmony and simplicity itself.

Garden design	Christopher Bradley-Hole, London, GB
Location	London, GB

New ideas from ancient roots

Boxwood, it is said, was prized by the ancient Greeks. Today, in spite of its tiny, almost invisible flowers, and the mildly poisonous alkaloids present in its leaves, this evergreen, with its dense, hard wood is still one of our best known and loved shrubs. Kitchen gardeners use it for edging, while more formal designs favor box as a strong structural element. It also often appears in the French and Italian palace garden designs of the Renaissance period. More recently, box has found itself in the spotlight yet again in the innovative designs of Belgian landscape architect Jacques Wirtz. He has created evergreen living sculptures from boxwood, which stand many feet tall, and are clipped into shape and "composed" by hand.

The garden

This garden was created on behalf of the English magazine "Gardens Illustrated" by two designers. Dutch landscape architect Piet Oudolf is internationally renowned for his contemporary designs with perennials and grasses, and English designer Arne Maynard is known for his imaginative, empathetic creations. This design uses box in a variety of ways. Established box trees have been clipped into rounded shapes and positioned closely together in a cloud-like formation, to form a living hedge around the perimeter. In sharp contrast, the central feature consists of evergreen cubes of box regimented one behind another, each set with a stainless steel fountain The impression is that plant and fountain are a single unit. The cloudlike box trees in the background are allowed to grow relatively unchecked, while the cubes are sharply squared off by clipping 2 or

3 times a year and are much denser, with shorter shoots. Oudolf's influence is apparent in the perennials astrantias, salvias and Jupiter's beard, which come as a welcome break from the evergreens.

Box: the best varieties; hints and tips

- *Buxus sempervirens* var. *arborescens* is the tried and trusted hedging variety with a dense growth. Box can grow to a very old age, and left unchecked, will reach heights of 13 ft (4 m) or more.
- *Buxus sempervirens* 'Blauer Heinz' has attractive, dark foliage, is slow growing and compact, and displays a good resistance against disease.
- *Buxus sempervirens* 'Rotundifolia' is a good all-rounder, thrives in shade, and once established, displays good drought-resistance.
- Tips: The best time of year for annual pruning is the end of May/ beginning of June. New shoots can be cut right back to the old wood. If the shoots begin to die back, fungal disease may possibly be to blame. Sometimes this can spread to the whole branch. Prune out affected parts immediately. The boxwood leafminer attacks only the tips of the leaves.

Garden design — Piet Oudolf, Hummelo, NL, Arne Maynard, London, GB

Location — London, GB

Dinner's ready!

Summertime in the garden can be synonymous with barbecue time. Picture the scene: the barbecue trolley is hauled out of the garage or basement, or a disposable barbecue is hurriedly purchased. The charcoal is lit under the intense scrutiny of the guests, and the food is ceremoniously cooked, well-seasoned with good advice. More advanced barbecue chefs, with a more adventurous repertoire than steak and sausages, might use a top-of-the-range appliance, a 'Weber' perhaps; some have a permanent grill in the garden, a brick-built barbecue corner. The new trend for outdoor kitchens is something else altogether. It provides an opportunity for everyone to lend a hand in preparing their meal and is an exciting new way to entertain.

The garden

The kitchen is the heart of the home, as the saying goes. So why not install a kitchen in the garden? With a cooking station in pole position, no-one need miss out. Such was the premise of this garden, designed by Philip Osman. A rustic, country-style kitchen would have looked old-fashioned – an elegant design is more stylish and better suited to this garden. Philip Osman created a garden for the whole family, with a kitchen at its heart, where comfort and convenience are not compromised: a gas hob, for instance, can cook anything from an egg for breakfast to a celebration dinner. Stainless steel work surfaces and pans require little maintenance. Vines clamber up a stainless steel pergola, continuing the theme. The most commonly used kitchen herbs grow in containers within easy reach, ready to be freshly added. Once the cooking is done, the garden also provides a comfortable eating area, incorporating a large table where everyone can sit down together to enjoy the meal they have helped to prepare. Even the ground – gravel interspersed by hardwood boards – looks bright, and draws the visitor in, as does the cheerful planting in front of the protective wall. The garden, with the kitchen as its focal point, is there for friends and family. Its appeal will endure as long as we enjoy cooking together. Then we can say that the investment has truly been worth it.

Alternatives for the "heart of the home"

- The outdoor kitchen is a combination of several individual teak units with zinc work surfaces. By Weishäupl: www.die-besten-gartenmoebel.de.
- The garden kitchen is a modular construction made from native acacia wood with stainless steel and Corian work surfaces. By Schaden Living Spaces: www.schaden.co.at.
- The mobile garden kitchen is a foldaway unit incorporating a table, a variety of Gaggenau hobs and appliances (teppanyaki plate, wok burner, induction hob, griddle and refrigerator). By MGM cases: www.mobilegartenkueche.de.

Garden design	Phillip Osman, Swindon, GB
Location	London, GB

A place of refuge

As a rule, designers and engineers draw inspiration for their work from the world around them. The natural world is fundamental to their creativity and development, the starting-point for countless new ideas. The recently-coined term "bionics" (a word derived from a combination of "biology" and "technical processes") refers to the application of systems found in biology and nature to the principles of modern technology. Scientists and engineers, architects and designers all find a common point of reference in this new discipline. Garden designers too are now using this concept in their work. Starting with a naturally occurring or artificially generated feature, they incorporate it into an innovative design in an exciting, new context.

The garden

What do straightened rivers and garden design have in common? A good deal, according to designers Marcus Barnett and Philip Nixon, who are both known for their modernist, unpretentious style. These river landscapes are like a mirror image of today's society, with all-too-familiar consequences. Barnett and Nixon have taken the concept of straightened rivers (a current trend in southern England, and, unfortunately, elsewhere) – albeit in an abstracted form – and used it in their design for a country garden. Thus we see the dramatic juxtaposition of hard landscaping with soft-textured perennial planting. Pools of water measuring some 5 ft (1½ m) wide cut across substantial seating areas. A series of four bridges, each measuring 25 ft long by 3 ft wide (7½ x 1 m), feel pleasant underfoot, and connect the different areas of the garden. They are made from western red cedar, with galvanized metal edging. Low concrete walls set with flint and, unusually, also topped with wood, frame the spaces. Large, roomy furniture designed by Philip Nixon and manufactured by Jeremy Long, is ideal to relax in, and works perfectly in this geometrically strong design. The two designers resisted the idea of a tropical hardwood, preferring instead to use Canadian western red cedar from the giant conifer *Thuja plicata*. After a sunny summer season, the wood will take on a silvery gray color.

The plants

The yellow daisy-like *Doronicum × excelsum* 'Harpur Crewe' is, sadly, not particularly well-known, but its clear, precise blooms are almost more impressive in early spring than the better-known coneflower *Rudbeckia fulgida* 'Goldsturm' is in high summer. At 16 inches (40 cm) high, it mingles with *Nepeta × faassenii* 'Walker's Low', a variety of catmint which if cut back occasionally, will keep flowering right up until autumn. Dotted through the design also, albeit a little hidden, we find alumroot *Heuchera cylindrica*, with its tall stems of yellow-green flowers.

Garden design   Marcus Barnett, Philip Nixon, London, GB

Location   London, GB

The power of light

It is easy to underestimate the importance of appropriate garden lighting. We tend to install emergency and security lighting to help us find our way up and down steps, to the front door and to the garage, and then leave it at that. Or we might think about motion detectors: lights that switch themselves on the instant they perceive a threat – or a cat on the prowl! And not forgetting ambient lighting, which makes the darkness around the house as bright as day. What is meant here by appropriate, and what has, thankfully, become fashionable, is additional lighting with no practical purpose; lighting designed to take the edge off the darkness, to break through the shadows and to be easy on the eye; in short, to bring new life to the night garden.

The garden

This house, with its distinctive silhouette, comes into its own every evening with the use of a well-thought-out series of halogen lights. The lights vary in brightness to emphasize the architectural elements of the building, where light and dark combine to paint a balanced picture. Notice how this theme continues into the garden. The interaction is perfect; treetops and towering branches are picked out, as well as some smaller bushes and flowers. An extra dimension is added as light reflects off the surface of the swimming pool. To the right of the picture, the glass footbridge, an integral part of the pathway around the garden, is lit up from underneath.

Garden design and implementation   Thomas Heumann, Weinstadt, Ger
Location   Weinstadt, Ger

An obvious relationship

The idea of living and working under the same roof is deeply attractive; it saves time and is environmentally responsible. If we were to keep a tally of the time we spend in the car, bus or train traveling to work over a lifetime, it can add up to months, or even years. It is a statistic which has given rise to a new trend developing a new generation of industrial and trading estates. These are proving ever more popular with employers – to the point of wanting to live on site. Of course, that is not always a good thing: being so close to work, one is always available, and bit by bit, the boundaries between professional and personal life are eroded.

The design

A suggestion to build a wall between the private garden and the delivery area for this surface refining business was met with some disapproval – the space had, until now, been used for growing vegetables. Initially there was opposition from the client, who felt that a hedge would be just as good, natural and, in fact, more attractive. However, having taken just one night to think it over, he came to the right decision, and the contract was duly awarded. There were still compromises to be made, however: not only was the wall to be completely separate from the house (which was part of the plan in any case) but the gap between them had to be wide enough for the boss to slip through to take a short cut to work.

The garden

The original intention was to paint the wall off-white and make it a focal point. Unlike planted hedging, this would look good in all weathers. It was the client's idea to use color. The different shades created by this ragging paint effect combine to make a breathtakingly beautiful, living blue color. At nearly 16 ft tall and 8 ft wide (5 x 2.4 m), it certainly draws the eye. Next to the well-used garden on the other side of the wall, with its patio, pool and blue accessories, this zone is designed to be practically maintenance-free. A few individual plants are dotted around, but the dominant features are the huge shell limestone rocks brought in from a nearby quarry. Their flat surfaces positively invite you to sit down. The ground is laid with chippings of the same stone – easier to maintain than a lawn, or even the neighboring orchard (on the right).

The planting scheme

The narrow gap between wall and house is filled with an American arbor-vitae (*Thuja occidentalis* 'Smaragd'). In front of the wall is a spherical box bush, and to the right, a clump of zebra grass (*Miscanthus*), which will reach a height of some 5 ft (1.5 m) by late summer. The crown of the beech tree (*Fagus sylvatica*) in the foreground will one day be pruned to make a box shape, echoing the shape of the blue wall, but it will be some years before this can happen.

Garden design and implementation   Hans Fahrion, Notzingen, Ger

Location   Notzingen, Ger

A walk-in room installation

For a sculptor, the garden is a space in which to mount an installation. The open space behind or in front of their house becomes an integral part of their art. Plants cease to be naturally or deliberately positioned objects, but are absorbed into the artist's work. The garden is wholly designed by the artist, and becomes part of the art experience; a new experience every day.

The garden

When Gisela Glucker and Jürgen Hauff moved in some 20 years ago, the garden was in need of a complete architectural makeover. It had previously been used purely to grow vegetables in a bid for self-sufficiency. The intervening years have seen a complete change. A few heads of lettuce still grow here and there, and there are box hedges in the background, but on the whole, the garden, which lies directly in front of the studio, has become sculptor Gisela Glucker's living and lively art installation, a work in progress. She likes to use the English word "artificial", preferring it to her native German equivalent; the sound, she says, is melodious, and evokes the qualities of friendship and artistry. Analogies with music and painting are welcomed; the garden is a picture, painted using plants and objects. The base for Gisela Glucker's installation is carefully-sized river gravel, and the dominant color is ultramarine, which rarely occurs in nature. The color plays an important part in the installation: the red content of ultramarine makes the blue appear warmer – fiery even, and has an immediate impact. Used as a foil for variegated foliage, the effect is misty and atmospheric, rather like an impressionist painting. In the presence of dark green foliage, however, the ultramarine reveals its deep midnight blue component. On the extreme right, we can see panels of wood salvaged from demolition sites and mounted onto steel posts like placards, acting as a marker in the garden. At their base, Japanese sedge (*Carex morrowii* 'Variegata') enters the picture, in beautiful counterpoint with the green box bushes behind them. Seeing this juxtaposition in terms of a musical progression rather than a prosaic planting scheme is typical of the artist. The melody progresses via a hummock of blue glass before finally resolving into ultramarine. A spherical shape is still discernible in the hummock; it dissolves at an angle of 45° to eventually become one with its river-gravel base. A pair of masonry slabs with ultramarine sides defines the space and draws the eye towards the paving stones, the fragments of hedging, the clipped robinia and the towering maple beyond. Gisela Glucker sees her installation differently every day, in every light. This is the advantage of accessibility. Her husband, Jürgen Hauff, is happy to pitch in. He is indispensable in realizing her vision – he carries her, she supports him. However passionate one is about art, an installation of this stature can neither be created nor enjoyed alone.

Garden and color concept   Gisela Glucker, Tübingen, Ger

Location   Tübingen, Ger

A new kind of garden room

There is something compelling and mysterious about the black holes in our universe, mainly because they have not yet been explored. They remain an enigma. Not so the black holes in this garden – or more precisely in the pool. They, too are full of mystery, and demonstrate an individual new approach in the field of garden design.

The garden

A patio does not always have to be directly outside the living room. Why not have an attractive outdoor space at the office, where workers can take a lunchbreak, or relax for a moment when the end of the day still seems a long way off. Even smokers have a right to some outdoor space! Sink down into one of these comfortable loungers, and you are guaranteed a fascinating glimpse into a wonderfully imaginative garden. The planting scheme is varied. A more detailed view of the perennial borders and the pool is afforded from the solid oak cubes (17½ x 17½ x 17½ inches; 45 x 45 x 45 cm), which are introduced at different levels, first of all forming a path through the plants, before leading away to the edge of the pool. They function well as seating. The garden's most innovative feature, however, is the sequence of square "black holes" in the pool, whose positioning in the water echoes the cadence of the oak cubes. Like the black holes in the universe, they are strangely compelling.

Garden design	Andy Sturgeon, Brighton, GB
Location	London, GB

A meadow in the backyard

What is a garden? It is, quite literally, an enclosed area of land where plants are grown, with varying amounts of intervention. It can be used to grow fruit and vegetables (a kitchen garden); or with some creative input, it can be used solely for rest and relaxation (an ornamental garden). The idea of a kitchen garden is slowly coming back into fashion, so today's gardens are usually a combination of the two. Growing your own vegetables, however, is not proving as popular as growing your own fruit.

The garden

This plot is out in the country, and it is big. The everyday part of the garden, the part used most frequently, is closest to the house, with its flowerbeds and pool, wisterias and white borders. An opportunity arose to purchase a neighboring plot of land, and the resulting in-between area has been skillfully developed. Inspiration came from the formal Italian parks of the Renaissance period and from the French 18th century predilection for classical styles, so a fruit orchard was planted. The standard trees are not yet fully grown, but in a few years the owners can look forward to harvesting plenty of delicious fruit. The planting includes apples, pears, cherries, plums and mirabelles. A crabapple tree grows nearby, whose fruits are not for human consumption; they are a major source of food for songbirds. Any fruit left on the branches makes an attractive seasonal decoration for the home. Each tree stands at the centre of a rectangle measuring some 20 ft x 10 ft (6 x 3 m). In a classical garden, these would have been squares. There are three rows of trees altogether. In their present youthful state, the trees make less impact than the juxtaposition of wild meadow and 6 ft (2 m) paths of closely mown grass. The artistic effect of this is breathtaking; the long grass sways in the wind, casting soft shadows in the evening sunshine, and can rival the beauty of the burgeoning young crops in the fields all around. To be effective, the grass paths have to be mown once or twice a week, with precision, keeping to exact lines. A paving stone in each corner keeps this from being a haphazard affair. The meadow grass is trimmed once or twice a year with a scythe, particularly just before harvest-time, to avoid windfalls sinking into the grass and remaining hidden.

Meadows with grass paths

This stunning effect can be achieved in any garden where an area is laid to lawn. It also conveniently cuts down on weekly mowing! Grass can remain undisturbed at the base of the trees, creating attractive, wild areas. Another idea is to make islands of meadow within a lawn, and plant them with spring flowering bulbs like tulips or crocuses.

Garden design   Fenna R. Graf, Ascheberg, Ger

Location   Ascheberg, Ger

Isn't it magic?

Fairytales, myths and legends are not an obvious choice as the basis for a garden design, but this was the theme for the Schloss Ippenburg Garden Festival; the design brief was to create a garden in keeping with the theme. Not a feel-good garden, then, complete with patio and comfortable seating, but rather a tantalizing treat for the eye.

The concept

What is real, and what is just illusion? Take off on a flight of fancy. Use the magical powers of circle and sphere to open yourself to the power of nature. It was Heraclitus who said that everything is transient, everything flows past. But does everything really flow? It looks like water, but is that glittering pool really water? And what is that shimmering green on the path? And what is happening to those hoops? They seem to sink into the green and blue grass, one after the other, finally to disappear into the pool. Then there are spheres of all sizes and textures. The tallest are the bluish green spheres of Lawson's cypress, whose dramatic trunks tower high above the hedge border. Even they seem to be sinking into the ground! Isn't that a reflection, right there in the centre of the pool? And something has dissolved into particles of light. Or could that be the spheres of box, changing, shifting; standing to attention one minute, soft and comfortable the next, like a family group. It is magic!

The garden

The aim was to turn the 100-square-foot space (30 m²) within the hedging maze into a garden room filled with a myriad of magical objects, all in shades of green and blue. The starting point was a blue pond; a pool filled with thousands upon thousands of fragments of glass. Four lofty Lawson's cypresses (*Chamaecyparis lawsoniana* 'Alumii') rise up from this imaginary pool, their trunks at different heights, partly above the beech hedging, but they are not alone. Next to them, a row of hoops, each a different shade of blue, jump out of the "water" then dive back in, each deeper than the next. The illusion is perfect – some of these hoops are simply reflections. In the midst of the hoops, a disco ball adds even more glitter when the sun shines. The box spheres, arranged on one side as a family group and on the other as a neat row, echo the shape of the disco ball. The planting is low-key, complemented by blue fescue 'Blauschwingel' (*Festuca cinerea*), newly planted and still a little limp, African lily (*Agapanthus africanus* 'Headbourne') and by a spiraling strip of lawn. Just the chunks of green glass left now. They exude an air of otherworldliness, sparkling secretively like oversized crystals (crushed glass by Otto A. Müller Recycling GmbH, Hamburg; www.oam.de).

Garden design   Ulrich Timm Grünplanung, Hamburg, Ger
Location   Schloss Ippenburg, Bad Essen, Ger

A voyage of discovery

The Japanese have this style down to a 'T'. A typical Japanese tatami room has several windows, only a few of which are opened at any one time, affording the visitor a limited view of the garden. Which windows are opened depends on the season and the appearance of the plants: a good way to sustain interest in the garden.

The garden

Young garden designer Janine Crimmins has taken the Japanese pattern as a basis, and modified it for her design. The concept of restricting the view is not a new one, but here, it has a fresh, contemporary feel. Why allow everything to be seen at once? A voyage of discovery is infinitely more exciting. Janine Crimmins has built a high wall dividing the garden into two areas, each with very distinct characteristics. In the foreground, we see the chaotic garden: sage, feather grass (*Stipa tenuissima*) and South America vervain (*Verbena bonariensis*) grow from between the stones as if by accident. Then, through a large cut-out window behind all this chaos, we see an orderly garden planted with fiery colors: helenium 'Moerheim Beauty', yarrow (*Achillea* 'Terracotta'), dahlias 'Bishop of Llandaff', and tufted hair grass (*Deschampsia* 'Goldschleier') all grow in front of segments of red wall, broken up effectively by yew trees (*Taxus*), and, in the centre, by water cascading down a slate pillar. Our curiosity is awakened, and that is no accident.

Garden design Janine Crimmins, Stockport, GB
Location Tatton Park, GB; from fall 2007: Cheshire Fire & Rescue Service Headquarter, Wainsford, GB

26

Bowling along

A planting scheme usually starts with a solid framework of wood. Trees and woody shrubs come first, followed by roses and perennials. Grasses are often included, but bulbs come a long way down the list. This is a pity, as bulbs are an attractive addition to the garden. This applies to tulips and the very early flowering spring bulbs, such as snowdrops, daffodils and crocuses, but equally to bulbs which flower later in the year, when the garden is already full of foliage. Ornamental onions (*Allium*) belong in this category. For years, these beautiful flowers had been viewed with some derision, but now at last they have found favor again, and occupy an important place. The allium family does not consist purely of ornamentals, however. Garlic, chives and even wild garlic, today's culinary must-have, belong to the same family. It is not surprising, then, that these flowers all give off an unmistakable smell of onion.

The garden

Do you prefer a formal garden, a show garden or a themed garden? Anja Maubach's delightful nursery and garden center, Arends Maubach (established in 1888 by her great grandfather), offers both "plants and garden architecture". Among the swathes of perennials, there is no shortage of flowering bulbs. The broad path is interspersed with squares of houseleek, and flanked on both sides by one of the loveliest types of ornamental onion, *Allium* 'Globemaster'. They increase in number year upon year, as the bulbs propagate by producing young offsets which flower the following spring. As with all plants in the onion family, the foliage is unattractive, dying off as soon as the flowers form, so it is a good idea to hide it away behind a screen of perennial planting, or simply to cut it away, taking care not to cause any damage. The plant is attractive long after the flower fades; even the seed-head adds interest in a mixed border.

Ornamental onions: attractive, tall, frost-hardy varieties

- *Allium* 'Globemaster' is fast becoming one of our most important plants. Its round head is made up of tiny star-shaped flowers providing architectural interest when left to dry after flowering.
- *Allium sphaerocephalon*: These reddish purple flower heads are smaller, opening up in July/August.
- *Allium* 'Purple Sensation' is a very attractive variety of ornamental garlic.
- *Allium* 'Mount Everest' has a beautiful round flower head of purest white.
- Planting tips: allium bulbs should be planted in October or November. Their foliage has an unattractive tendency to turn brown before the flowers appear; this can be hidden by judicious perennial planting. Plantain lilies (*Hostas*) are good for this purpose – they provide the perfect backdrop for the alliums' swaying heads.

Garden design   Anja Maubach, Wuppertal, Ger
Location   Wuppertal-Ronsdorf, Ger

A feast for the senses

To experience a garden fully, we need to awaken all our senses. Give it a go – it can be tried in every garden. Look and listen carefully, touch and smell. If all our senses are satisfied, the design is a good one. It means that the garden works well in terms of layout and planting, and that man can be at one with nature in this small area.

The concept

This garden is a very special place, both beautiful and stimulating. It is a place to be alone, or to spend time with friends and family. Water is paramount here, as it connects strongly with our senses, flowing gently through the entire space. The central seating area is housed on an island accessed by a footbridge. The water can be experienced in various different ways; in its beautiful reflections, its subtle sounds, its light, its tranquility, its coolness. It is even pleasing to the touch, an opportunity to refresh and revive. The layout is linear, but with notable contrasts. Six ornamental vines rise up from the pool, although vines do not usually crave water, thriving in warm, sunny climes. Sun-drenched plants flank the terrace and lead the eye towards the copper-tree, a modern sculpture in the background. This is a bubbling water feature by Tora Harmsworth, centrally positioned in its own raised pool, also in a copper surround. Just behind it, we find that most important garden feature, the open-air bar, here fashionably furnished with woven cane (Hularo) the color of mocha (Cane-Line Collection). The decking is made of thick oak planks, while the footbridges are narrow-gauge stainless steel grating. These starkly contrasting textures encourage visitors to engage all their senses to appreciate this highly unusual garden.

The plants

The stems of the common grape vines (*Vitis vinifera*) have already become woody; they are about thirty years old. A crop of sweet grapes, however, is not the point here. Rather, they are prized for their gnarled trunks, their twining branches and their distinctive foliage. Naturally, the vines are not planted in the water, but in individual beds, open at the bottom, and framed with brushed steel. There is, of course, also a selection of true water plants. In the foreground we see a pretty clump of pickerel weed (*Pontederia cordata* var. *Lanceolata*), with its charming sky-blue flowers. The panicled flowering stems of the common water plantain (*Alisma plantago-aquatica*) cannot compete, and neither can the fluffy heads of the umbrella grass (*Cyperus alternifolius*), a rush-like marsh plant, which can also be grown as a houseplant, and is not frost hardy.

Garden design   Vanessa Adorni, Ellenbrook, GB
Location   London, GB

Precision behind the house

Knowing where to begin is the most difficult part. Where does one find the perfect creative design, one which suits the plot and is still in keeping with the house; a design of which the designer will be proud, and which may even bring him recognition? And so the sketching begins; an endless realm of possibility. Designing your own private garden can, however, be even more problematic. Not so for Marc de Winter. It takes a good deal of courage to do something completely contrary to expectation, but he sees it as his prerogative to be unconventional. He is a landscape architect, but also an artist.

The garden

When Marc de Winter first moved here, there was no garden to speak of, just a few elderly fruit trees. There is no reason, he decided, why a garden should have a patio, a lawn and some mixed borders, particularly when seen from an artistic point of view. Using his artistic license, he decided to place a long beech hedge on the garden side of the house, with three rows of box trees in the foreground, one row the shape of tenpins, the other two rows shaped like slightly flattened bowling balls. Each is more than 3 ft (1 m) in diameter. The bowling balls are identical, leaf for leaf. Not a single plant is out of place. Only the elderly fruit trees are left to grow unchecked.

Garden design	Marc De Winter, Bloem Bloem, Halle-Zoersel, B
Location	Halle-Zoersel, B

Today´s *gardens*

Fit for fun

Gone are the days when a swimming pool was only used for swimming up and down, in an effort to keep fit. Nowadays, anyone who values their leisure time, has enough space and can afford a bit of luxury would no doubt prefer this "swimming garden", particularly on a hot summer's day.

The garden

This garden is unusual in that it provides a total solution. The plot is fairly large, and offers both a swimming pool and a shady seating area which goes one step beyond the idea of a classic pergola. The two together form a cohesive, if rather unusual, unit. The different levels add interest. The pool is not built into a sun-soaked terrace as we would normally expect, but extends lengthways from beneath the roof. A flight of floating sandstone steps connects the two levels. There is a choice of seating: a secluded spot amidst the fresh green foliage, or up a couple of steps to the large airy terrace, shaded by the plastic slatted roof. The pavilion is lavishly built using composite timber frame and sandstone flooring. It serves one other significant purpose: one side affords a refreshing view of the turquoise blue water, the other looks out over the cheerful planting scheme. It all makes for a wonderful holiday atmosphere.

Garden design	Andy Sturgeon, Brighton, GB
Location	Chelsea Flower Show, GB

Activity pool

When it comes to choosing between a traditional swimming pool and a natural one, opinion is divided. Some favor the eco-friendly alternative with its softer water, others prefer clear, chemically cleaned water, whose temperature can be regulated to provide comfortable swimming conditions all year round, but this consumes energy, and can prove quite expensive. A natural swimming pool is usually esthetically more pleasing in a garden setting, but it requires more space. The surface area of a natural swimming pool needs to be about one-third greater than the actual swimming area, depending on the filtration system used; the additional space is needed to accommodate the biological regeneration zone and water filtration system.

The garden

When this passive house, with its state-of-the-art heat retention and recovery systems, was still at the planning stage, the owners decided to include a natural swimming pool, and to install it right on the terrace, where traditional designers would have been more likely to plant a rose garden. They wanted to be close to water, both to look at and, weather permitting, to bathe in. Although the children were still young at the time, the parents did not consider the pool a potential hazard. 5-month-old Lara attended a baby swimming course and learned how to behave in and around water. She now happily swims laps around the pool, and enjoys long summer days splashing in the water (under supervision). The overall area of the pool is around 325 square feet (100 m²), half of which is available for swimming. The bathing season begins in May, and by summer, water temperatures can reach 77 °F (25 °C).

Algae and mosquitoes

The pool attracts dragonflies, beetles, birds and, at spawning time, also frogs. Algae can grow, as they can on any natural expanse of water, but the flora and fauna keep mosquitoes at bay.

The pool

The pool is divided into two sections: a swimming area about 10 ft (3 m) deep, and a shallower regeneration area where the plants grow. A concrete barrier wall under the water separates the two. This particular pool has an even shallower paddling area. The water throughout is biologically purified using plants. Underwater planting includes pondweed (*Potamogeton*) and ditchmoss (*Elodea*), while above water level we find marsh plants such as arrowhead (*Sagittaria*), pickerel weed (*Pontederia*) and bulrushes (*Typha*). The plants are specially chosen to ensure that the water stays hygienically clean and clear to the highest possible standards. A surface skimmer (as used in a traditional pool) skims debris off the surface, while a pump circulates water (Biotop Landschaftsgestaltung Ges. m. b. H., www.swimming-teich.com).

Garden design	Eveline Merkinger, Amstetten, A
Natural swimming pool	Biotop Landschaftsgestaltung Ges. m. b. H., Weidling, A
Location	Amstetten, A

An ideal combination: a self-cleaning pool is the perfect partner for this eco-house with its ultra-low energy outgoings.

Full potential realized

Owners of small gardens may often cast envious glances at larger properties in more spacious grounds. The idea of working with a large space and all the flexibility it offers may seem very tempting, but this should not prevent us from exploiting the full potential of our more modest gardens. With some creative thinking, even a few square feet can be turned into an unusual, imaginative garden. We just have to try a little harder.

The garden

It is not always easy to find a creative solution for a garden situated behind a house, not least because the logistics involve traipsing through the house with plants and materials. Good balance needs to be achieved in a relatively small space, and the natural light may be compromised by high walls and fences: nobody wants to be overlooked by their neighbors. It was not difficult for the owners here, both art lovers, to decide on a design concept. They were not interested in a planting paradise, but rather a relatively spacious outdoor room where they could entertain friends and family. When the designers suggested erecting a wall with vertical slits to provide a visual barrier, and painting the walls a dusky pink, the clients were convinced. It is not a color they would have chosen themselves, but in this context it is exactly right. Pink brightens up sad, gray, walls, and acts as the perfect foil for anything placed against it. The courtyard garden is full of interesting little details. A second level has been introduced, the upper level being something of an art gallery. The designers also wanted to provide a focal-point; they suggested a formal pond with a wall behind it, the opening filled with slate. This creates the illusion of deeper water in a wider pool, and breaks up the expanse of pink in a very elegant way. Natural Portland stone has been used for the pool edging and steps. The bench in the foreground is also of Portland stone, which has been polished. The ground cover is toned beige gravel, bordered by widely spaced rows of stone setts. The two bronze sculptures, designed by the garden designers and built by Dennis Fairweather, provide a sharp contrast, as does the avenue of tall, slim-trunked pyramidal hornbeams (*Carpinus betulus* 'Fastigiata'), and the blossoming medlar.

The plants

The beautiful medlar tree (*Mespilus cydonia*), in blossom here, but weighed down in fall with yellow fruits, towers over the mainly dark-leaved perennial ground-cover plants: alumroots (*Heuchera micrantha* 'Palace Purple'), sage (*Salvia officinalis* 'Purpurascens'), and fennel (*Foeniculum vulgare* 'Rubrum'), with lady's mantle (*Alchemilla mollis*) in the foreground.

Garden design   Fiona Lawrenson, Haslemere, GB; Chris Moss, London, GB

Location   London, GB

A seat in the sun

Two crucial factors in creating a garden design are location and environment. This can mean anything, from the architectural language of the buildings to the needs and desires of the clients, but mainly it is taken to mean the surrounding properties and land. It may not be easy to take it all into account, but it is essential to do so, as a garden is influenced to a huge extent by what goes on beyond its boundaries; the trees, the walls, the buildings and the neighbors. If the plot is large, it is even more important to create a distinctly individual atmosphere.

The garden

The boundaries of this garden, set in the balmy sunshine of California, seem to be fluid. There are no tall trees; the vista and freedom are boundless. This seemingly endless space was particularly important to the design of the swimming pool with its outdoor seating area. In keeping with the character of the terrain, the designers built low concrete walls to retain the soil and to give a sense of order and neatness to the poolside area. These create an interesting angular design at different heights, and effectively subdivide the space. The clean lines of the pergola cast sharp shadows, and echo the structure of the house; they are a fine example of transparent architecture in the garden. The result is a setting so tranquil one hardly dares to disturb the warm, inviting depths of the pool.

Garden design	Chandler & Chandler, Napa, USA
Location	Napa Valley, USA

A new esthetic

Gardens are becoming increasingly complex; we demand much more from them than we used to, including a greater degree of comfort. They are stylized, rather like a film set. There was a time when the largest available area would have been given over to lawn; this idea was subsequently dropped in favor of a garden pond. Now, in an effort to stay up-to date, we would have no qualms about installing a swimming pool or reflecting pool in the space.

The garden

This garden is dedicated to the pursuit of enjoyment. The outside world stays very firmly outside. The main purpose of the white walls is to keep the real world out – the only gap is filled with a yew hedge. A seating arrangement under the pergola is the focal point here, and is the only part of the garden to be made of wood – American pine to be precise. A relaxed style of building adds to the holiday atmosphere. The seating space is in the open shape of a 'U'. A slatted wooden roof, some 7½ ft (2.30 m) above the decking provides some shelter from the sun's rays. A sail which lowers at a slight angle is designed to keep off the worst of the rain during summer showers. A double batten construction with broad spaces between the beams lightens the rear wall and keeps it from feeling oppressive. Three stylized poppies are featured on a wall-hanging which breaks up the area and draws the eye up above the outdoor sofa. The 16 x 10 ft (5 x 3 m) decking area is exactly the same size as the roof, and is broken up only by two structural wooden posts. The garden falls away on either side of the seating area, adding to the effect of being on stage. It seems to hover over the water, while

giving affording a good view over the welcoming gray color of the granite flags. The square reflecting pool has been positioned with care to create a stunning effect. 16 ft (5 m) square, and 1½ ft (50 cm) deep, the pool is lined with black pebbles, making it appear deeper than it actually is. The pinnacle, however, is the lovely waterfall which cascades gently from the front of the terrace into the pool. A stylish addition.

Details

Attention to detail has helped to achieve good balance in this garden. Slabs of natural Chinese gray granite have been laid with care. The steps are finished with a gentle overhang, which makes them easier to use and esthetically more pleasing, while the paths are edged with 16 x 8 inch flagstones (40 x 20 cm) punctuated by a middle strip of 8-inch squares (20 x 20 cm). This pattern is repeated throughout the garden, showing that the design has been well-thought-out and correctly executed.

Garden design   Jamie Dunstan, Rotherham, GB
Location   Tatton Hall, GB

Old meets new

What relevance can the parks and gardens of yesteryear have for contemporary garden design? Not a great deal at first glance. But in reality, there is a noticeable tendency to revisit traditional designs and old values. It is an approach worth considering, as many of the old ideas are quite ingenious, and could certainly add interest to gardens today.

The garden

The ideas incorporated into the redesign of this inherited garden seemed a little pedestrian at first. A straight line was to be created along the longest diagonal in the garden, making it nearly 200 ft (60 m) long. The line was to lead to a pavilion built in the style of a Greek temple – the temple of Apollo in Bassae, in fact, one of the most impressive temples in ancient Greece, close to the village of Andritsaina. Using a highly detailed plan, the façade has been reduced exactly to scale, and measures some 20 ft (6 m) across. The skillfully built replica even includes pillars and Greek urns. To catch the eye, a parterre was introduced in the middle of the garden between the house and the temple – an idea that can be attributed to the highly fashionable designs of Prince Hermann von Pückler-Muskau (1785–1871). Landscape architect Hans Dorn developed the parterre as a large 30 ft (9 m) square. To right and left, three planted squares stand one behind the other, yet linked together. Between them, the eye is drawn to another three squares, lawn this time, bordered almost imperceptibly by slabs of sandstone. The planted areas are framed by low-growing box hedges, and a second green hedge forms another link. The planting is masterly; it consists of a single swathe of South American vervain (*Verbena bonariensis*) in each square, at once structured and relaxed, attracting countless insects to its tufts of purple flowers atop 3 ft (90 cm) stems. An alternative, should fashionable white be the color of choice, would be the spectacular feather reed grass (*Calamagrostis × acutiflora* 'Karl Foerster') together with shasta daisies (*chrysanthemum maximum* 'Gruppenstolz'), annual white cosmos, and the feathery –leaved Mexican aster (*Cosmos bipinnatus*). In addition, the landscape architect has used an ingenious device which almost goes unnoticed. The garden is built on a slope which he decided not to align – not least because of the upheaval this would cause – so although the lines are horizontal, they are not actually parallel. The visible hedges and the central sandstone frames are set at an angle which the eye does not at first perceive, and which lessens the contrast. Another trick: the lower hedges are dark green yew (*Taxus*) rather than box. In comparison, the paler green of the box-bush squares looks lighter and brighter.

Garden design   Hans Dorn, Frankfurt, Ger

Location   Schlüchtern/Elm, Ger

Perfect symmetry

What sort of garden would suit original art-nouveau architecture? A classical design perhaps? Or something innovative and unusual? Expect the unexpected in this garden. Clean lines replace curved paths and sweeping swathes of planting; we see straight lines, angular raised beds, and a surprisingly limited selection of plants. Not only are the hard landscaping materials low in cost, they are also few in number. Could this be a new kind of thrift, or does it mark a return to simplicity and lack of fuss? The tranquil atmosphere is a welcome contrast to the stresses of everyday life, to sensory overload of every kind. The effect is one of simple beauty.

Clean lines

The new tendency towards restraint can be demonstrated in any garden; size has little bearing. The effect can be achieved in a small urban garden by using just a very few focal points. Just one eye-catcher should suffice. In a larger garden, restricting the main design to a single line of vision from the house would produce a similarly unexpected effect; one avenue of trees, or a solitary group of flowering shrubs, for example. Or how about a single specimen tree, a slim, angular pool, or a themed garden? A space dedicated to vintage roses, perhaps, or to blue-flowering perennials. Limiting planting options pays dividends in almost every case.

The garden

Surrounded by tall houses and gardens with towering overgrown shrubs, this little piece of land was choked with moss, and in dire need of a makeover. In collaboration with an architect friend, a plan was drawn up which incorporated only straight lines – almost as a reaction to the current state of the garden. The inspiration was the long living room, stretching from the front of the house right to the terrace at the back. Its rectangular shape is echoed in the gravel areas, flanked on both sides by raised beds planted with fish-pole bamboo (*Phyllostachys aurea*) and white busy lizzies (*Impatiens*). The space is laid with fine gravel from which twelve cube-shaped box bushes emerge, underlining the symmetry of the design. The narrow central strip of garden again echoes the long, narrow living room; a carpet of stonecrop (*Sedum*), edged on each side with planks of hardwood. The back of the garden enjoys the most sunshine, making it a natural spot for the seating area. It is paved with ordinary concrete flagstones. Visual barriers per se were not essential in this garden, as the overgrown shrubs in neighboring gardens provide a good degree of privacy. A straightforward boundary marker was quite enough – a fencing screen with a lattice pattern was chosen. The end result is an attractive, pleasing garden, whichever way one chooses to look at it.

Garden design   Michael Hartmann with Dr. Heiner Schaub and family, Hannover, Ger

Location   Hannover, Ger

Great inspirations

There are many ways to design and develop a magnificent park or garden – but it is essential to be in tune with the genius loci, the protective spirit of place. This is a fundamental design principle which states that designs should be adapted to the context in which they are located, in terms of both space and time. A good understanding of the client's needs and wishes is also paramount. Successfully choosing a basis for the design, be it a theme, a motif, a structure, a color or combination of colors, is a leap forward in the process, as is accurately pinpointing the client's priorities. A central idea will usually emerge, around which the initial design, the choice of materials or even the color scheme can be developed. We need to keep a firm grip on this thread of an idea if we are not to be distracted by a maze of temptations and limitless possibilities, and if the design is to remain consistent. As far as this particular contract was concerned, the history of the location was not a factor – it was built on the neutral foundation of a show garden. However, the client was absolutely clear about what he wanted.

The garden

This was not to be a run-of-the-mill design. This was a request to realize a dream; to design a garden echoing the shapes and colors beloved by English painter Simon Carter. His paintings are characterized by a forceful use of color together with rough textures: fiery orange, shades of blackcurrant and fresh green were all to be transposed into a landscape context. Garden designer Thomas Hoblyn explored the plant world for living equivalents, and came up with a discreet carpet of lady's mantle (*Alchemilla mollis*) with fine filigree flowers reaching up from its foliage combined with neatly upright dark blue monkshood (*Aconitum carmichaelii* × 'Arendsii') and the 5 ft (1½ m) tall salad burnet (*Sanguisorba tenuifolia*). The interaction of color is, however, less important than the sweeping sense of movement created by the design. A semicircle of tall, slim espalier lime trees stand in a sunken hollow no more than 3 ft (1 m) deep, echoing the elliptical shape of a classical amphitheater. Steps are set into the slope. Pure grass-green is the dominant color; any lawn-mowing difficulties are played down. Emerging from this background we see a cluster of Himalayan birches (*Betula utilis*), their white bark seeming to glow in the light while their canopies echo the lime-green of the grass, a perfect contrast. The wooden surface provides further contrast; it is not so much a functional terrace as another sweep of color, an effect enhanced by the play of changing light and shadow. The overall result was a resounding success – the garden was awarded a gold medal.

Garden design   Thomas Hoblyn, Bury St. Edmunds, GB

Location   Hampton Court Palace Flower Show, GB

The slim trunks of the espalier lime trees form a framework around the sunken amphitheater; a semicircle of white-barked birches cast dappled shade.

An outdoor living room

It seems that all too many urban gardens are nothing more than playgrounds, or else they are doomed to neglect. The seeds of landscape design rarely fall on fertile ground in this area. A pity, because a garden can create a strong bond between the house, the living room and the terrace. We have to look at it every day, so it is a worthwhile investment both in terms of new design ideas and cost, and should be recognized as such.

The garden

This garden looks big at first glance – a beautiful picture, not an urban back garden at all. Of course, this is the desired effect: one of Stephen Woodhams' trademarks is utilizing every inch of available space. The surroundings are deliberately shut out; this photograph shows almost the entire garden. Just visible in the foreground is the wooden terrace leading from the conservatory. Two wooden steps, which can also be folded up for storage, lead down to the main garden area, a space 26 ft long x 20 ft wide (8 x 6 m). On either side of the terrace stands a 2½ x 2½ ft (80 x 80 cm) sandstone trough, planted with a spiraling yew (*Taxus baccata*). The effect is completely symmetrical. The lower level consists of a gravel parterre broken up by a path of sandstone flags, which also frame the pool in the background. A furrow has been left in the centre of the path, and is planted with a strip of box, giving the impression of a boundary hedge right in the middle of the garden. Each side is bordered by raised beds planted with bamboo (*Phyllostachys*) and the evergreen Japanese spurge (*Pachysandra terminalis*) as groundcover. The ubiquitous water feature is a must-have in gardens today. Here water bubbles from a free-standing wall, over a highly polished sill and down a sheet of glass into the pool below, to stunning effect. The wall enclosing the pool doubles as a bench seat, a place from which to view the house and conservatory from a different perspective. Bring on the gin and tonic!

The lighting

This garden provides interest all year round: the strong design, the evergreen planting and the water feature are not seasonal. Strategic lighting can heighten their year-round appeal. The lights have been skillfully chosen and positioned: small, low-voltage halogen lamps are used to illuminate individual plants and features. More info from Büro für Lichttechnik R. Noelle, 24576 Hitzhusen, www.nightscaping.de.

Garden design   Stephen Woodhams, London, GB

Location   London, GB

A glass summerhouse

Summerhouses have their own unique character. They tend to be sited at the back of the garden, so they are closer to nature, but they can also be positioned to provide a focal point from living room or terrace, or to be more discreet altogether, peeping out from behind a swathe of flowers, shrubs and rambling roses to spellbinding effect. Summerhouses are available in all shapes and sizes, from rustic wooden frames with thatched roofs to much fancier architectural styles, including art nouveau or classic tea pavilions. A summerhouse is generally a small building with a roof, sometimes heated, sometimes not; it can also be a simple, open structure with metal supports swathed in climbing plants. Golden rain (*Laburnum*), actually a small tree, provides a particularly distinctive natural camouflage, especially when the long flowering racemes trail into the building. But a word of warning: laburnum is highly toxic.

chatting late into the night. A footbridge connects the house to this light, bright garden room. A couple of steps lead down to the garden itself; the difference in levels adds an extra dimension. A piece of advice: mosquitoes can be a nuisance mainly in places where water levels change, often in natural wetlands, which become breeding grounds in warm weather. Contrary to popular belief, this is rarely the case in pre-formed pools.

The summerhouse

A summerhouse made of glass is unusual; it is more expensive and more difficult to erect than the usual wooden structures. When an architect and the director of a construction company build something for personal use, we must expect the unexpected; something modern and contemporary. He and his wife decided on a glass structure, which, being only some 20 ft (6 m) from the house, also takes on the role of conservatory. The woodland backdrop is charming, and the structure seems to hover over the water. True, it is nothing fancier than a pre-formed pool, but the effect is magical. An added advantage is that mosquitoes tend to stay away from this sort of pool, even when family and friends sit

Technical specifications

- Dimensions: 14 x 14 ft (3.99 x 3.99 m)
- Height at eaves: 7½ ft (2.3 m)
- Angle of pyramid roof: 40°
- Vertical supporting posts: 2 x 2 inch (50 x 50 mm) solid profiles
- Roofing profiles: T 50 structural steel profiles and 2 x 2 inch
- (50 x 50 mm) cladding profiles
- Roof bracing: umbrella system, iron flat-bar connected to vertical posts with steel wire rope
- Bridge and summerhouse flooring: grooved hardwood, untreated

Garden design   Friedrich C. Meyer, Jever, Ger

Location   Jever, Ger

More architecture, please!

Garden designers try to serve two masters: their design has to appeal to the client, but it must also be in keeping with existing architecture. These are not necessarily conflicting requirements; they should be mutually complementary.

The garden

This courtyard garden is much like any other in that it is heavily influenced by the architecture of the surrounding façades. This particular house, designed by Spengelin and Lutz and built in 1973 was meticulously restored by Dieter Neikes. It is strongly reminiscent of the Bauhaus movement of the 1920s, a style which introduced a new, modern approach to the world of architecture. The garden area continues in the same vein, successfully echoing the architecture inside. This is not to say that more individualistic pieces are banned; they are positively encouraged, and prevent the garden from becoming a relic of the past. As far as possible, the inner courtyard is paved with bright shell limestone flags, each measuring a generous 3 x 3 ft (1 x 1 m). This works well; it gives an even grid pattern with criss-cross jointing. Notice how the area incorporates three different levels, both for added interest and to give greater visibility to the planted areas. The Corten steel raised beds with their trademark rust-colored appearance add a modern touch. They are set at a slight angle, to help soften the harsh geometric lines. The use of evergreens such as box and yew (*Taxus*) is a further device to lessen the severity. A group of four Indian bean trees (*Catalpa bignonioides* 'Nana') sets the scene for another seating area, and also links the courtyard to the garden outside. It is

echoed by a tree of heaven (*Ailanthus altissima*) whose feathery leaves cast a dappled shade. The ambience is calm and tranquil – as much of a pleasure to gaze at from the living room as it is to sit in.

About CORTEN, also known as Corten steel

CORTEN is a steel alloy which forms a rust-like patina when exposed to the weather. First patented by American BD Saklatwalla in 1932, it was subsequently developed and produced by the United States Steel Corporation. The name is based on its two main properties: CORrosion resistance and TENsile strength. CORTEN steel is suitable for riveted, screwed or welded constructions and is frequently used in an architectural context, where it is valued for its distinctive color. It is also a popular material for use in sculpture.

Design   Friedhelm Hellenkamp, Inspired by Nature, Icking, Ger

Location   Hannover, Ger

A minimalist approach

Clear the clutter and concentrate on what matters! It takes a lot of determination to limit the number of materials in a design and then to stick with your decision, but the result makes it all worthwhile.

The garden

The brief was unambiguous; the clients wanted a garden which echoed the colors and materials used in the home, and which stood out from its neighbors. Gray was to be the dominant color, with accents of black and white. Stainless steel was the material of choice, along with basalt. Black comes into play when the basalt is wet.

The concept

Symmetry is the watchword here, and stainless steel. The 36 ft long x 4 ft wide (11 x 1.2 m) stainless steel pool follows exactly the same line as the front and patio doors. From the entrance door, the eye is automatically drawn to the bright red wall from which the water flows. Gleaming metal spheres lie on the surface of the water, which is only 4 inches (10 cm) deep, making for a light, relaxed atmosphere. The 6½ ft (2 m) tall wind-sail is made from perforated stainless steel, and is attached to its pole with a ball-bearing joint which allows it to turn in the wind. The furniture, too, is made from pure steel (L. Heinen, www.edles-aus-edelstahl.de), as are the lights, the mast for the fabric sun-sail and the plant-bed surrounds, which are set into the ground to frame the box bushes. Smooth Vietnamese basalt paving stones (5 x 5 x 3 inches,

14 x 14 x 8 cm) are used for the terrace and laid in a checkerboard pattern. The same stone is used as edging around the pool, to maintain a feeling of continuity. Luminous sets of identical size are inserted at intervals. In place of a lawn, the owners have chosen a surface of basalt chippings, in keeping with both the minimalist concept and the color scheme.

The Plants

Two plant species define this space: box and bamboo. Box spheres flank the water. The plan specifies 16 x 16 x 16 inches (40 x 40 x 40 cm) "cushions" of box. The box hedging in front of the wind-sail also needs time to develop. It will be another two years before the bamboo (*Fargesia murieliae* 'Smaragd') planted against the fencing panels at the rear of the garden will be tall enough to provide a green framework. There is no perennial planting here. The focus is on clean, architectural lines which really come into their own when darkness falls and the luminous sets are switched on.

Garden design   Ute Wittich Gartenarchitektur, Frankfurt, Ger

Location   Frankfurt, Ger

A breath of new life

Until a short while ago, this was one of those ubiquitous tired, old gardens, established long before exposed aggregate concrete and railway sleepers made their mark. Patios were laid with multi-sided tiles of red Weser sandstone, as was the fashion. A pond, incorrectly constructed and subsequently silted up, resulted in a boggy area in the middle of the garden. Older gardens need to be looked at carefully to determine which features are worth saving: the pond was not. Older trees can grow to be unusual specimen plants, even in unfavorable conditions: they grow almost unnoticed amongst the other plants, but then, when the undergrowth is cleared, we see them in all their glory. It is never advisable to transplant established trees, as their root-balls may not be able to withstand the stress: far better to leave them where they are. Young trees in a nursery have their roots managed in a different way, making them more resilient. The same is not true of azaleas, yew, laurel and rhododendrons, all of which have been successfully re-positioned within this garden. Azaleas and rhododendrons respond best, and are most likely to thrive.

The garden

The new owners bought this 50-year-old property some ten years ago. After a period of extensive modernization to the house, their attention turned to the garden, which could no longer remain as it was. Redesigning it was not easy; the various terraces and garden doors were on three or four different levels. Municipal parkland forms the backdrop. This works in its favor, not only because the mature trees are naturally attractive, but because the area will never be developed. A minor drawback is that as the trees grow, the hours of sunshine enjoyed by the garden will decrease. Changes in the garden allowed for more seating areas, linked together by a path. Light brown clinker bricks and slate tiles had been used in the construction of the house, so this color scheme was carried through into the garden. Local basalt was sourced from the nearby Eifel Mountains and used for the steps and supporting walls (palisades measuring 8 x 4 x 60 inches (0.2 x 0.1 x 1.5 m). A gracefully curving pathway which leads around the garden to a further seating area was laid with 3–4 inch (8–10 cm) basalt pebbles. A low box hedge bordering the path to one side is an excellent way of emphasizing the sweeping curve of lawn and path. All other paths are paved with beige concrete flags measuring 16 x 16 inches (La Strada 40 x 40 cm), while the hard landscape areas either side of the raised terrace (on the right of the photo) are laid with gravel of the same color. The planting scheme features mostly shades of green, with box, rhododendrons, ivy and frost-hardy camellias. A flower garden full of roses and herbaceous perennials would not do well here; the tall trees provide a peaceful, tranquil environment in which only shade-loving plants will thrive.

Garden renovation   Michael Zanders, Viersen, Ger

Location   Viersen, Ger

New, hard landscaping materials: basalt, pebbles and pale concrete bring fresh color to the old garden. On the right: a charming specimen magnolia tree.

An outdoor lounge

Here we see new developments in garden seating. Any garden feature sited away from the house needs to provide visual interest when viewed from the terrace. It needs to be inspiring and inviting. New ideas are always welcome.

The garden

This ground-breaking design is by young Australian designer Jack Merlo. Clearly, large-scale designs are feasible wherever space allows – and this is a case in point. The design incorporates a very generous seating area, built as a single unit together with the lap pool, and even includes a fireplace for chilly evenings. The use of a sweeping curved surface to define the area, rather than a barrier or wall, makes for an even more spacious feel. This is a device often used by photographers to express a sense of space, although they would usually use white. Even the anthracite-colored pool is visually extended using this technique. The whole unit is a distinctive pale-gray color, with walls and partitions in a contrasting dark slate-gray. In an unexpected touch, the seat seems to float above the water. A smattering of shadow offers protection from the midday heat. Note the planting combinations echoing the clean lines of the pool area. European hornbeams (*Carpinus betulus* 'Fastigiata') are set in a carpet of dwarf sweet box (*Sacococca hookeriana* var. *humilis*), both planted together in a raised bed on the lawn.

Garden design   Jack Merlo, Brighton, AUS

Location   Chelsea Flower Show, London, GB

Excellence squared

When a house is sold and new owners move in, they usually embark on a program of renovation in which the garden is often included. The new owners may have different tastes; they might be younger, they may have children; their priorities might simply be different. The move is an opportunity to evaluate the existing situation, scrutinize the planting, and introduce radical changes if necessary. In this case, it was essential.

The garden

First of all, the house was renovated. Then the owners built a glass extension to house the kitchen and dining room. At last it was time to turn their attention to the garden. The house stands on a slight incline, with a busy road nearby. The first priority was to plant a hedge of European hornbeam (*Carpinus Betulus*) to block out traffic without obstructing the view of the surrounding countryside. It was the starting point for this cozy garden room; and now the time had come to plan the swimming pool. The pool was carefully designed to make the garden appear larger than it actually is. The water surface measures some 72 x 26 ft in total (22 x 8 m), with a seating area at its heart. A number of design techniques have been used to good effect: the water level is 1½ ft below that of the house, giving a more attractive view from the dining room, and at an angle which gives the observer a fine view of the reflections off the surface. It seems to bring the outside in. The eye is drawn spontaneously to the water in the pool, and does not compete with the view beyond. The two terraces look like natural extensions of the house. There is an area for sunbathing and another for eating, relaxing and

sunbathing. The retaining walls and generously sized concrete flags, 2½ x 2½ ft (80 x 80 cm) are pure white. They bring light and brightness into the garden, even on cloudy days when the pool cannot be used.

The plants

- Two square beds in front of the dining extension have been densely planted with box, clipped strictly to a height of 16 inches (40 cm). At the centre of each stands a Japanese maple (*Acer palmatum*).
- The whole space, including the pool, is screened off with European hornbeams (*Carpinus betulus*). Regular pruning keeps them neat and slim. Field maples (*Acer campestre*) rise above them. In two or three years' time, when they have knitted together, the trunks will be trimmed to a height of some 6½ feet (2 m) to act as a tall hedge.
- In the background to the right of the house we see a lovely old crab-apple tree (*Malus* 'Red Sentinel') with its long clusters of fruit.

Design   Kristof Swinnen, Sint-Niklaas, B
Location Sint-Niklaas, B

Welcome to Scandinavia!

Is there such a thing as a typical Scandinavian garden? Scandinavian interior design has been shaping our tastes for some time now, but does this extend to the garden? Can we see any Swedish influences outside? Such were the questions posed by students of landscape architecture at the University of Hannover, and the answer was a resounding "no". Plenty of big-name companies and products promote a positive image of Sweden, for example Ikea, H & M and Volvo – but there is no gardening equivalent. It is high time one was introduced!

The idea

It was essential for the design to reflect Sweden's national identity and progressive attitudes. Sweden is famous for its innovative products, its enlightened attitudes towards design and music, and its magnificent scenery. A large area is covered by water, mainly in the form of lakes, and about half of the country is made up of forest and natural woodland. The design needed clear definition, with no blurring of stylistic edges (an example of blurred edges would be a Tuscan koi-carp pool in the grounds of a thatched cottage).

The garden

The design concept picks up three different themes. Firstly, the planting: a row of white-barked Himalayan birches (*Betula utilis* 'Doorenbos') stand at the ready, to welcome the visitor and accompany him in. Closer to the ground, ferns and bearded iris (*Iris*-barbata-eliator-hybrids) form a relaxed group representing Sweden's natural woodland. Behind the terrace is a row of Swiss mountain pines (*Pinus mugo* var. *mughus*). The second theme touches on surface and texture. Old-style gardening is represented by a lawn (hardwearing grass mix, for sport and active use). An aluminum pool, 1 x 3 ft in size and 8 inches deep (4 x 1 x 0.2 m) with welded joints and grooved edging represents not only the watery landscape, but the country's advanced manufacturing capability. A bed of polished 'Black Beauty' granite cobbles gives an icy, glacial feel, while two clumps of decorative Chinese silver grass have been positioned in strict symmetry among them to represent the coast. The third theme is the living space. It, too, has its own symmetry; the seating area is paved with 'Oriental Black' granite slabs, 12 inches wide, but in varying lengths, echoing the shape of the lawn, to symbolize Sweden's harmonious relationship with nature. The 'Dr No' chairs are by Philippe Starck. The boundary has been left open in places, reflecting the Swedes' openness and hospitality.

Visitor's tip: "Smal_land, a modern Swedish Garden" was created for the Park and Garden Country Fair 2007, where it was awarded one of two first prizes. The 25 x 16 ft garden (7.5 x 5 m) has remained in place, and is available for viewing at Stockseehof (www.park-garden.de).

Garden design Timon Graf, Sven Ninnemann, Maximilian Holzhausen, Laura Winter, students of landscape architecture at Hannover University, Ger

Location Park & Garden Country Fair, Stocksee, Ger

A cage full of stones

Despite the fact that concrete products have improved over the years, today's gardens are using more and more natural stone, often in innovative ways. Perhaps it was simply that up until now, stone has never been seriously considered, but now landscape architects and their contractors seem less constrained in their work with natural stone.

The concept

Just a few years ago this would have been unthinkable: the boundary wall in this garden has been built using gabions. The very word gabion was once only recognized by a select few; now it has become a fashionable way to build a garden wall, even when there is no incline to secure. In this garden, the wire mesh baskets are 3 x 1½ x 1½ ft (1 x 0.5 x 0.5 m) and contain layers of Yorkshire sandstone. A contrasting layer of color comes courtesy of a Venetian red marble mortar compound, while the white layer is etched glass. The materials are mutually complementary. A French limestone footpath leads in a sweeping curve around an expanse of water – the garden's dominant feature. A perfect solution was found to access the path from the wooden decking (see right). In the foreground, the focal point is a cube of sandstone topped with a crown of box (*Buxus* 'Tide Hill'). There is more sandstone behind, this time sliced into smaller slabs and built up into a right angle. On the other side of the curving path is a plot of Chinese silver grass (*Miscanthus sinensis* 'Gracillimus'). These are not marsh plants, though. In fact they are not planted in water at all, but in perfectly ordinary soil. That leaves the metal construction. Like a pergola, it echoes the garden's structural elements, its curves and right angles; it provides a visual link between the gabions and the water, casts shimmering reflections on the surface and enhances the secure, enclosed feel of the garden.

Natural stone in baskets

Gabions are wire mesh baskets, usually galvanized, which are filled with stones. Depending on their function, they can measure up to 13 cubic feet in volume (4 m³). Historically, they were used to secure slopes and inclines at the side of roads, for example, to help prevent landslips. In these cases, they were built up either vertically, or following the angle of the incline. Nowadays they are also used as walls and pre-fabricated components. In vineyards, dry gabion walls are increasingly replacing dry-stone walls. The mesh baskets can be filled with whatever stone suits the purpose.
Gravel is good value, and we can see that stone slabs can be used in garden settings; if not throughout, then at least in the visible areas (see photo).

Garden design	Christopher Bradley-Hole, London, GB
Location	Chelsea Flower Show, London, GB

Under glass

Nowadays, the term "glasshouse" tends to conjure up visions of a conservatory. But even the smallest spaces in the garden can be enclosed in glass, becoming eye-catching in their own right. This includes cloches. Cloche is a French word meaning 'bell', and denotes a shaped glass structure used to over-winter tender plants, or to protect seedlings and young vegetables in spring. Here is an English variation on the theme.

The garden

English designer Peter Marston was among the first to have a lasting influence on the design and construction of conservatories, in Germany and elsewhere. He is occasionally asked for advice about landscaping and planting the area around one of his glass structures, and he has some very innovative ideas. The space between house and conservatory (in the background on the right) has been divided into three, linked by a flagstone path: a lawn area, dramatically planted with birch trees, a still pond and a patio paved with pale-colored limestone (sandstone). The 8-inch deep pool is framed with aluminum and painted black. Even the basalt stones are completely unobtrusive. Marston proves that glass can look attractive as a garden feature with these four glass cylinders, each containing a papyrus sedge (*Cyperus*) Each provides a micro-climate to sustain the plant. The glass needs to be cleaned occasionally inside and out, to keep these mini-glasshouses looking good all summer long.

Garden design   Peter Marston, London, GB

68   *Location*   Chelsea Flower Show, London, GB

Complete concentration

Whatever your garden layout, its themes, styles or priorities, it is essential to include at least one area of calm. The teachings of Buddhism can be applied effectively to garden design, and the practice of Feng Shui is no longer limited to homes and indoor spaces, but also includes the garden. And what better to introduce at the centre of your peaceful space than a statue of Buddha performing a mudra? It is arguably the ultimate calming influence.

The garden

This garden-within-a-garden was created specially for the vivacious owners of this property. The boundary along the side has been planted with a beech hedge, and right at its mid-point, a small area has been set aside as a space for calm reflection. It slots neatly into the 6½ ft (2 m) wide bed of closely trimmed box with its inset square of four standard box trees. To draw the eye, the area creeps forward a little, claiming some 12 inches (30 cm) of the grass area. The border between the lawn and pebbled area is carefully and clearly delineated. This quiet zone was added recently, and introduces a valuable air of tranquility. Buddha is at the centre, with his gesture of greeting and reverence, radiating peace and strength. Two upright box trees (*Buxus sempervirens* 'Rotundifolia') serve as a backdrop, emphasizing the solitary figure, while also protecting it. Calmness abounds. Each of the flat beach pebbles is unique, yet together they seem to be equal. The only relief comes in the form of a specimen box tree shaped like a bonsai. The two oil lamps really come into their own at dusk, when their flickering flames radiate an unexpected feeling of strength. The stresses of the day evaporate; annoyance and agitation dissolve into nothingness – and all because of a small statue of Buddha.

Buddha and Feng Shui

- A statue of *Buddha* embodies the need to focus inwardly, as well as on the spiritual path of meditation and enlightenment. Buddha is portrayed in various postures and with different hand-gestures, each of which carries a different meaning. And we must not forget the big-bellied, laughing Buddha, who, it is said, is responsible for our cheerfulness.
- *Feng Shui* is a system of teachings from the Far East, the practice of which can bring harmony to our homes, both indoors and out. Feng Shui literally translates as "wind and water". Its purpose is to optimize the flow of energy; Chi, the life force, needs to travel in gentle curves; its flow is blocked if angles are too sharp. The Bagua is like a grid overlaying the garden. It is divided into nine zones, each representing a personal value such as family, career, wealth and helpful friends. The "knowledge and wisdom" sector covers calm and contemplation. Buddha enhances this, and strengthens it. At the centre of the Bagua is the Tai Chi, the Supreme Ultimate.

Design Manon Mengers, Hamburg, Ger
Location Hamburg, Ger

Recycling and ethical design

The idea of reusing raw materials in our gardens is still in its infancy. There are a number of tried and trusted methods: composting works well, and shredding twigs and branches to make mulch is also widely accepted. The use of crushed glass as a mulch shows promising results, while colorful garden furniture made from post-consumer plastic waste is at an early stage of development. Sadly, fair trade is still not the norm, and the idea of fair pay for a fair day's work is little more than wishful thinking. Hopefully it will soon be a matter of course.

The garden

This show garden demonstrates what can be done to construct and enjoy a garden with a clear conscience. The walls by the terrace door are built from gabions – galvanized wire mesh baskets filled with stones. Here, the baskets are filled with concrete and sandstone rubble, attractively built up in layers. The walls are almost 20 inches thick (50 cm), and can store the heat of the sun all day, releasing it gradually in the evening. This produces, in effect, a beneficial micro-climate. The same type of re-claimed stone can be used to build steps, as we can see in the background. A flagstone laid on top increases stability. The wall-cum-seating and the stepping stones "floating" over the water are built up from granules of recycled glass – not a material we often see as yet. The decking is wood, hardwood to be precise, sourced from an ethically managed, environmentally responsible forestry plantation, and certified by the FSC. The Indian sandstone, too, is ethically sourced and produced in accordance with the Ethical Trading Initiative (ETI). Sandstone pavers are set into the decking to follow the line of water flow from the waterfall by the terrace gate to the point where it enters the pool. It leaves a bright, white path, adding interest and lighting up the dark-colored wood. This simple effect hides a very clever device: the water is not simply circulated; it is filtered through a bed of regenerative plants such as reeds (*Phragmites*) before being pumped back into the irrigation pool.

The plants

- A plot of trumpet lilies (*Zantedeschia aethiopica* 'Crowborough') and flag irises (*Iris pseudacorus* 'Ivory') brightens the marginal area between the irrigation pool and the low wall.
- The large, maroon-colored leaves of the golden groundsel (*Ligularia dentata* 'Desdemona') echo the color of the wooden terrace. Clusters of dark orange flowers appear in summer.
- Rodgersia (*Rodgersia podophylla* 'Rotlaub') with its shaped, purplish leaves adds drama. In summer, creamy white flowers emerge above the foliage.

Garden design — Scenic Blue Team, Faversham, GB
Location — London, GB

Welcome!

The appearance of the front garden, or in fact of any entrance area be it the home or office, is of the utmost importance. It needs to be functional, yet inviting. A path is essential – a good width is about 4 ft (1.2 m), and unexpected touches in the planting work well. One also needs to consider access to the garage or carport, the position of the doorbell and post-box, and a discreet space for dustbins. A long pathway, or a concealed entrance door are added complications. Skilful design is needed to make the area more interesting and to entice the visitor, even if access is tricky, or involves steps.

The garden

What did the owners do to make their front garden and the pathway to their house so enticing? This used to be a gas station, so the whole area had to be thoroughly cleansed and sanitized. A difference in ground levels of nearly 3½ ft (1 m) did not help. The first task was to build a retaining wall around the front garden area. The steps and pathway were skillfully made into a feature. At the point where the steps lead up, cement slab walls were faced with a brilliant white layer (Dyckerhoff Weiss), while the surrounding gray slabs were given a polished terrazzo finish. Warm reddish-brown ('Rosso Verona') was used for the steps themselves, which were slotted, at right angles, into the retaining wall. This created a separate entrance zone paved with a broad strip of flagstones – the ideal place to position two tall, slim zinc planters. The path to the house leads through a modest avenue of hawthorn trees (*Crataegus* 'Carrierei'). A seating area on the left is well-protected by a 3½ ft high (1 m) yew hedge

(*Taxus baccata*). The slim-stemmed standard wisterias, eight in total, are a spectacular sight, especially when in flower. Even later in the year they are a delightful addition to this unusual front garden.

Growing wisteria

A wisteria that refuses to flower season after season is a familiar problem for many gardeners, and one that can often be remedied simply by judicious pruning. The best way to start wisteria is from cuttings, or as a grafted cultivar. Plants raised from seed are identical in appearance but have a different genetic structure, which means that it may be many years before they bloom. All types benefit from pruning soon after flowering. Wisteria flowers on the previous year's growth, so care must be taken in summer not to prune back the shoots with developing buds, but to remove unwanted side shoots. If necessary, the leading shoot can be cut right back into the old wood.

Garden design and construction Hans Fahrion, Notzingen, Ger

Location Wernau, Ger

Between heaven and earth

There would have to be a very special reason indeed to build a garden seating area above the garden itself. It may be that the views are better from such an elevated position, or perhaps because it is more secluded, away from the cellphone and laptop; the quality of the air may be better, or it might simply be the lure of something new and unusual. At the moment there is a trend towards building tree-houses in the strong branches of old, established trees; an adventurous project which can strengthen bonds between father and son. Tree-houses are available in kit form, but how much more satisfying to use materials found in your own garden. It encourages creativity and co-operation, and the end product is both individual and unique. Unfortunately, this garden did not have the wherewithal for a conventional tree-house.

A rather unusual seating arrangement

This 2-storey house was bought by the Seiler family a few years ago. Certain compromises had to be made: the house had no balconies, and there was no access to the garden. Balconies can be added on, which normally presents no problems, but the sunny side of the house overlooks a busy street with considerable traffic noise, while the garden side is too shady. The only way to go was away from the house, and into the sun. Architect Gabriele Mühler-Seiler hit upon an idea which seems crazy at first glance: to build an elevated terrace, almost like a raised hunting hide, accessed by a bridge from the second storey of the house. Far from being crazy, however, it has proved to be the ideal solution; everything on one level, 13 ft (4 m) above the ground.

The sun-deck

After considerable research, the designers concluded that to catch the best of the sun's rays, the seating area needed to be 26–33 ft (8–10 m) away from the house. But what shape should it be? Square, rectangular, round? Plans were drawn up, rejected and redrawn until suddenly a quasi-semicircle emerged, a sort of lens-shape, for want of a better description, rather like the hull of a boat. Accepted design practice usually echoes the shape of the existing buildings, but in this case the architect broke the boundaries and came up with something totally different, a complete contrast to the house. It was to be 26 x 13 ft (8 x 4 m) accessed by a 33 ft (10 m) bridge from the second storey apartment. The only material considered was stainless steel with a coating of iron mica, which had already been used in the renovation of the house. In contrast, the railings and floor are of Douglas pine. First of all, the decking and grid bridge were swung by crane over the house and into position. Then came the question of a sunshade, as it was obvious that something would be needed for hot, sultry days. A series of experiments determined the best angle for an awning which was then fixed to a rectangular frame and can be rolled up or down at the touch of a button. If it gets too hot upstairs, there is always another seating area underneath, on the ground.

Design   Gabriele Mühlen-Seiler, Baden-Baden, Ger

Location Baden-Baden, Ger

Just for fun

Not every garden owner has green fingers or even an overwhelming love of plants. A patio, a lawn and some low-maintenance planting will do nicely. The importance accorded to the garden can often be a matter of age and lifestyle. Children who grow up surrounded by nature tend to appreciate their gardens more as adults. We may not even be aware of our love of plants until we come to share the beauty of nature with our children, or to find that beauty for ourselves. When it comes to regular garden maintenance, even confirmed garden-lovers may find themselves pushed for time.

The design

Mark Ashmead was presented with a brief simply to design a low-maintenance garden for a professional couple who have little interest in pulling radishes or mowing lawns, pruning roses or spraying them. Their free time is severely limited, and they buy everything they need from the supermarket, including cut flowers for the home, so why would they need a flowerbed? What they want from their garden is a place to relax and entertain friends. It needs to be simple and spontaneous, with no complicated preparations, no moving heavy teak furniture; they sit wherever it suits them at the time, wherever the sun happens to be. Practicality is the key. The planting scheme is unspectacular for those who are interested, but also uncomplicated. Trees and perennials look so natural in their chosen places that one could hardly imagine them anywhere else.

The garden

Curves set the tone in this formal garden. A barrier wall, together with a tubular steel pergola, divides the space into two. At the front, with direct access from the house, is the entertaining area. Everything is in the round, including the steps leading from the house to the lower-level cobbled seating area by two different routes, and the curved seating itself, the focal point of the pergola. Three tall-stemmed hornbeams (*Carpinus betulus* 'Fransfontaine'), with an undergrowth of herbaceous perennials, define the zone in a very artistic way. Speakers have been installed, so that the transformation from garden to nightclub can be speedy. Between the boundary walls on the right, a path leads through to the quieter private garden. Here is a place to relax, to forget the pressures of everyday life. A garden does not have to bring extra work – it can be there purely for pleasure and enjoyment. That is enough to satisfy even a demanding garden designer.

Garden design   Mark Ashmead, Chelmsford, GB
Location   Hampton Court, GB

One for the boys

Men and women expect different things from a garden, and design accordingly. Clean lines and low-maintenance lawns compete with magnificent sweeping flowerbeds and rose-laden arches – at least in theory. Only a compromise solution would satisfy both, and allow everyone to enjoy the garden. Unfortunately, the compromise usually involves the woman contributing the inspiration and creative input, while the man is left to put her ideas into practice, either by financing the project, or by doing the sheer physical work: building walls, planting or felling trees, mowing lawns. Does such a marked gender difference exist in real life? Yes, it does to a certain extent. Gardens designed by female designers tend to have a more ornamental bias (with notable exceptions – see p. 56, for example). In this photograph we see a garden with no flourishes and flounces, one that need not worry about striking the right balance. This is a man's garden through and through: one for the boys.

The garden

The dominant feature in this unusual garden is the circular pool; it takes up a good half of the available space. The perfect geometric shape is carried through to the dual-level concrete and limestone seating area which hugs the rim of the pool. An elegant flight of steps, also in the round, leads down to the lower level. A waterfall under the decking and the stainless steel vortex overflow are attractive to look at, but also pleasing to the ear, as the water ripples away. The overall shape and layout have the enclosed feel of an amphitheatre or perhaps a Roman bath. Privacy walls add color, as do the blue shade-sails, which are probably more decorative then functional. Planed oak timber is used for the decking. It is the perfect foil for the stronger color. Here we see is a lifestyle statement for the younger generation. Designer Andy Sturgeon confirms that he "used materials which are familiar to men and come from places where we feel comfortable: health clubs, bars and fashionable restaurants". The garden is sparingly appointed and very much design-led. The few accessories are the work of well-known fashion designer Matthew Williamson. The space has the uncluttered, unruffled feel of a zen garden. Anything extraneous would distract the mind. Even the plants are just bit players. The steep inclines are planted with lawn-like creeping moss, their shape echoing the terraced seating opposite. This is not a garden for the ladies. They would no doubt soon be adding flowers here and there, then some soft furnishings and within a short space of time, we would see a complete transformation. But this is a garden for the men, and for the few short days of the Chelsea Flower Show, we should not begrudge them.

Garden design	Andy Sturgeon, Brighton, GB
Location	Chelsea Flower Show, London, GB

This part of the garden has been skillfully separated into a spa area for those who appreciate design and the good life. Relaxing to the sound of trickling water is indeed a pleasure.

Modern *components*

Art in the monastery

It is always possible to renovate the ruins of old buildings in keeping with their original style so that we do not forget the past, but new ideas can be more exciting. Each generation has a fresh approach and adds some of its own ideas. The same is true of gardens, although, of course, they are more transient. The end result, however, justifies the extra work.

The garden

If we decide to break away from the original style, why not try something completely different? Why not art, for example? In a bold move, Sonia Lesot and Patrice Taravella decided to experiment, and it has paid off handsomely. Inspired by the architecture of the Middle Ages, they created unusual works of sculpture in the grounds of an old French Monastery, the Prieuré Notre Dame de l'Orsan. They installed a temporary garden against a backdrop of the monastery's domestic offices. The background consists of close-clipped linden trees (*Tilia*), shaped to resemble a wall clad with evergreens, with openings for windows. In front of the wall is the garden itself. Except for one diagonal path, the whole area has been planted with wheat. Bamboo poles have been positioned in a pretty diamond pattern to enclose the space, and to edge the path. The ends of the bamboo sticks are capped with snail shells, which cast the most appealing shadows. This truly is art in the garden, and safe for children!

Garden design   Patrice Taravella, Maisonnais, F

Location   Maisonnais, F

82

Come on in, the water's lovely!

What a pleasure it is to redesign an existing garden, especially when the owners have just moved in, and have no particular rapport with the existing layout. With the emotional slate wiped clean, one can feel freer to experiment with new plans and ideas. A further advantage is that one or two mature plants can be retained and incorporated into the new design, giving the garden an air of maturity early on, even if the lawn is still a bit sparse.

The garden

There has always been a pond and swimming pool in this garden, ever since it was built, half a century ago. Both house and garden have been updated twice since then, most recently with a superb new layout. The design was based around the existing swimming pool, which was extended to create an impressive feature. The original pool was sited more or less between the jetty on the left and the ladder. A new angular design was developed, which absorbs the space in front to form a practical and attractive link to the terrace. A molded stone wall clad with strong protective fleece and sealed with waterproof film separates the 6½ ft (2 m) deep swimming area from the shallower planting zone. This pool uses the Teichmaster system, which aims to keep the planting zone relatively small – only 20% of the total surface area is used for filtration. These zones are present both at the front and the back of the pool, and recognizable by the planting of flag iris (*Iris pseudacorus*) and cattail (*Typha laxmannii*). The grating in the foreground prevents any contaminated water from the roof from entering the pool and compromising circulation. The steel gutters are an emergency measure in case of a downpour. The materials used are stunning, yet discreet. Extra strong concrete paving slabs, 25 x 12 x 5 inches (64 x 30 x 12 cm), and untreated larch wood give the garden a clean, contemporary feel.

Natural swimming ponds

The swimming area is 6½ ft (2 m) deep, and is divided off by concrete walls. A shallower filtration zone is built adjacent to the pool, and filled with marsh plants; it contains gravel and "Aqua Supertron", a granulate which encourages beneficial micro-organisms, and is planted with purifying plants such as cattail and rushes. A pump keeps water circulating through their root systems to be purified; it stays clean and clear with no further routine maintenance required. A skimmer is in constant use to draw debris from the surface of the water. The pool water is a closed-circuit system into which it is inadvisable to introduce any other source of water. For further information: www.teichmaster.de.

Garden design and construction	Hans Fahrion, Notzingen, Ger
Location	Kirchheim-Teck, Ger

The main event

A garden can touch us in different ways: it can be attractive and inviting, breathtaking even, or simply boring. But it is not often we feel exhilarated and amazed. This is something we can begin to expect more often, particularly as gardens are being slotted into unusual and underused spaces – an accessible rooftop perhaps, or a tiny courtyard. A range of components and effects can be used to appeal to our senses: unusual plants, unconventional materials, tactile surfaces, atmospheric lighting and exotic scents.

The garden

Philip Nash is not a man for cozy, romantic gardens. He likes to concentrate on the core elements, as he calls them, favoring clean lines, contemporary materials and architectural planting. While studying art and design, sculptor Philip Nash discovered a love of contemporary architecture, with garden design being an intrinsic part of this area. His background means he has a non-traditional approach to design and plant combinations, sees things more from a graphic point of view, and prefers a more spontaneous technique. This is a cutting-edge garden design, creating the garden as an experience where we should expect the unexpected. No lawn, no roses, no paving slabs, no wooden decking; instead we see glass, steel and light. This glass is like a stage in the middle of a showroom, lights casting inscrutable shadows on the still surface of the water. Wide steel beams (8 x 4 inches; 20 x 10 cm) surround the garden, enclosing the pond. The garden is accessed from a structured glass plinth which bridges the water. Turkish limestone, held in place by steel girders, makes up the terrace; the stone table is an unexpected feature, rising up from below the stage, supported by heavy glass sheeting. Two glass benches set among the plant beds continue this cool and perfectly linear theme, as do the cement-gray walls and the harsh fluorescent light pouring from their rectangular openings, in complete contrast to the soft LED lights on the water. An unconventional choice of plants echoes the garden's unusual architecture. A palm takes center stage, a role usually played by a specimen tree, a Chusan palm (*Trachycarpus fortunei*) to be precise. Behind it on the left we see one of the more attractive species of bamboo, *Phyllostachys vivax* 'Aureocaulis' with its upright stems (another correct term is stalks). The atmosphere of the pond area is lifted with an exotic plant selection: the blue-ringed aloe (*Agave Americana* 'Glauca'), planted in watertight containers, scouring rush (*Equisetum hyemale*), a throwback to the ice-age, and, on the extreme right, a yucca (*Yucca rostrata*) with its dense crown of narrow leaves. Even the top of the wall is planted: a green strip of tufted sedge (*Carex elata*) lifts it out of the ordinary. This is garden design breaking out of its boundaries; modern, architectural and artistic.

Garden design Philip Nash, Hampton Hill, GB
Location Chelsea Flower Show, London, GB

Exposed aggregates – a new perspective

As a finish, it has been around for a long time, and was particularly popular in the seventies. Just when it seems that the whole world is on the lookout for something new, and smoothly polished textures are flavor of the month, exposed aggregate rears its head again, this time in a new and updated version. This is no bad thing: it is a very versatile material, but this time around, we must guard against over-using it.

Exposed aggregate is a decorative concrete material whose surface has been removed to reveal the gravel or pebbles beneath. The most common way to achieve the effect is to apply a chemical retardant to the molding form to prevent the concrete from hardening at the surface. After curing, the unhardened matrix is removed by high-pressure washing. Although the aggregate was, and still is, usually gravel and crushed basalt, other materials and techniques are being introduced to bring this tried-and-trusted finish up to date, and make it suitable for even the most modern setting.

The garden

Here is exposed aggregate at its modern best, newly rediscovered for the contemporary garden. Exposed aggregate walls keep out the noise; the technique is echoed in the bench supports. They make a perfect backdrop. Uncommonly large pieces of flint have been used here, contrasting well with the pale gray of the concrete walls. Flint had fallen out of favor recently, and was merely a byproduct left behind when sorting pebbles, but times have changed.

Sharp angularity is becoming more fashionable than uniform roundness, and flint is no longer shunned. The flints in this garden came from the North Sea, off the East coast of England, where it occurs naturally in substantial quantity. The rocks are broken down to the requisite size for use as an eye-catching facing set into a rendered wall, or as exposed aggregate. The surface of the flint is so lively and uplifting that it adds interest even to a 6½ ft (2 m) garden wall. Elements of western red cedar wood and lavish yet relaxed planting meld with the elegantly unusual texture of the exposed flint walls to give a beautifully peaceful, modern garden.

The plants

The white flowers of the common foxglove (*Digitalis purpurea* 'Albiflora') are a highlight of the June garden, not least because of their height, but do beware, as they are poisonous. Since they are shade-loving, they prefer to hide in the background, although they are difficult to miss even there! Their somewhat smaller companions are the snowy woodrush (*Luzula nivea*) and the long-lasting blue flowers of the perennial catmint (*Nepeta* × *faassenii* 'Walker's Low'). Right at the back, next to the glowing white foxgloves, the slim trunk of a Lombardy poplar (*Populus nigra* 'Italica') adds structure. This moisture-loving tree reminds us of the North Sea coastline, home of the exposed flints.

Garden design   Marcus Barnett, London, Philip Nixon, London, GB

Location   London, GB

A puzzle garden

Planning a garden can be a bit like completing a jigsaw puzzle. If you find the right pieces and fit them together carefully, you wind up with a beautiful picture. The pieces here are the patio and paths, the flowerbeds, tree and hedges. Color is a major factor, as much in the hard landscaping – stones and steps – as in the leaves and flowers. Putting all these components together can be hard work, but if you treat it as a game, not only will you have more fun, but the design might be even better as a result.

The garden

In this garden, the designer plays on any similarities between its various components. He calls it a Hortus Conclusus, an enclosed space within which other smaller enclosed spaces are created. Eleven tall hornbeam hedges (*Carpinus betulus*) form the dividing walls. They are of differing lengths, yet their orientation is the same and they seem to interlock. The twelfth "hedge" is totally different: slim oak panels have been set vertically into a bed of gravel in a quincunx pattern, the pattern of five spots on a die. This was a common feature of early Arabian gardens. The fence panels form a partial barrier; the light wood adds an extra dimension to the attractively restricted views. The visitor can observe without being observed. The layout of the paths and ponds is also reminiscent of a jigsaw. Thin slabs of Italian basalt are skillfully linked together, echoing the narrow pools of water which are joined together by a canal system.

The paving stones seem to float above the water. The gray stone can become very dark when wet, so by way of contrast, the green of the grass and the beige of the gravel lifts and lightens the color scheme.

The plants

Lovely old-style shrub roses mix with luxuriant perennial planting and grasses. Included are: scented Gallica and Bourbon roses such as 'Louise Odier', 'Mme Isaac Pereire', and 'Tuscany Superb'. Perennials are chosen for their color, and include Italian bugloss (*Anchusa italica* 'Loddon Royalist'), snakeweed (*Bistorta officinalis* 'Superba'), red scabious (*Knautia macedonica*) and red trefoil (*Trifolium rubens*). The scheme is visually drawn together with a variety of grasses: tufted hair grass (*Deschampsia cespitosa*), blue moor grass (*Sesleria caerulea*), feather reed grass (*Calamagrostis × acutiflora* 'Karl Foerster') and, in the foreground on the right, giant feather grass (*Stipa gigantea*).

Garden design   Christopher Bradley-Hole, London, GB

Location   London, GB

The glass bead game

The range of surfacing materials for terraces and patios can be overwhelming. Choosing is not always easy, and tends to be a matter of feeling and instinct rather than a consideration of the costs involved. Should we go for something practical, or something with a warm, cozy feel? What color will suit the house? The choice basically comes down to natural stone, concrete or wood, or maybe gravel. Within these groups there are an infinite number of combinations, which only complicates matters. When finally the paving stones are delivered, stacked up and held together with rusty metal bands, our confidence can evaporate, and we can only hope that we made the right decision all those weeks ago; not just in terms of the appearance of the material, but whether it will suit our needs.

The garden

This small detail shows just what can be done to add color and life to a garden. The seating area is not made up simply of uniform paving stones; shimmering glass beads add another dimension. Even the path leading to the small pond with its shiny floating sphere has a style of its own. The three paving slabs have been cut away to form a concave shape at the water's edge, while small jetties jut out on either side. The steel forms are studded with glass beads in shades of blue, just like a mosaic.

Garden design   Alan Sargent, Ashbourne, GB

92   *Location*   London, GB

Striking a balance

We are lucky that nowadays we have access to a wider range of materials and fascinating new techniques than ever before. In our enthusiasm, however, we should remember that we do not have to try them all out at once. It is, of course, essential to try out new products and techniques and to observe the results, but in most cases, this is as far as we need go. When designing and constructing a garden, we only need to pick out what works best. This can also apply to the planting scheme. Palms and olive trees can be the right choice if that is what the owner wants. A garden should be designed with the needs of its owners in mind, not just to be visually attractive.

The garden

"The simpler the better", seems to have been the watchword of this famous landscape designer. The concept is crystal clear, and the garden radiates an enviable harmony. We can look at the garden from two perspectives: either we can see the large steel square as a focal point, or we focus on an island of lawn surrounded by calm, still waters and bordered by colorful planting with unmistakable Mediterranean influences. The overall impression is of peace and harmony. The first thing we see is beds full of oriental poppies, but if we choose to cross over the stepping stone to the almost-square lawn, we find ourselves in a different world altogether. There is a sense of excitement, yet the harmony persists, full of pleasing contrasts. The lawn area, with its set-in corners, is surrounded by a rill of still water. No goldfish or water lilies here, though. Six olive trees rise up from the water, as if they have been swimming there.

Their silvery leaves are an art form in themselves, evoking fleeting memories of vacations in the sun. They stand in the water in containers framed with galvanized steel. Steel is also the material of choice for the garden's main focal point, a huge metal square, with decorative mitered corners. Its open center draws the eye into the depths of the garden, framing a view of William Pye's Clearwater Cube water sculpture. Pietra Serena, a natural gray stone from Italy, has been chosen to complement both the olive trees and the steel. A few strong accent colors in the perennial planting balance the severity of the scene and lift the atmosphere.

The planting scheme

The olive trees (*Olea europea*) are planted on islands. They can withstand the mild English winters relatively easily, but may need frost protection in colder climes. It is worth experimenting with these trees, as they grow in such an interesting way. Tip: plant in spring, to allow the trees as much time as possible to acclimatize. The oriental poppy (*Papaver orientale* 'Orangeade Maison') is a real eye-catcher in spring, and is complemented here by yarrow (*Achillea* 'Terracotta') and wormwood (*Artemisia*).

Garden design   Arabella Lennox-Boyd, London, GB
Location   London, GB

Just a short way to go

Front gardens are all so different, and are used in such a variety of ways that they merit a book of their own (plenty are already available). But they are rarely a source of satisfaction for the owner. They are too big or too small, or have too little sunlight. There are however situations where there is no option other than to use the space between the house and the street as the main garden area. With a good, creative design, this can be a bonus – a garden where nothing is ever too far away, not even the kitchen.

The garden

Houses built at the turn of the last century have their own unique charm, but they tended to be pushed too far back from the street by today's standards, just for the sake of appearance. This house is no different. It would have been a pity to leave this space empty and under-used, so the landscape architects decided to make it into a feature, a kind of central meeting place. The biggest challenge was privacy, both visual and from ambient noise. The challenge was addressed in two ways: first, the garden was constructed two steps below street level, and second, to give privacy from the street itself, a lattice panel fence was erected at the boundary. A solid fence would have been inappropriate. Combined with the planting scheme, the lattice panel fence will form a natural-looking visual barrier within a few short years. The entrance gate is flanked by planted beds which also serve to conceal the carport in the background. The wall is constructed from sandstone blocks, linking it visually with the exterior of the house which stands on a sandstone base and has steps of the same material. The sandstone

used has been salvaged, and makes an attractive frame for the garden area. More seating is available if required for a larger gathering. This front garden space is subdivided into four "rooms". Two offer seating, one contains a rose-garden with square beds and box hedging, while the fourth is devoted to herbaceous perennials. The owners had to replace an existing apple tree: they chose a Japanese flowering cherry (*Prunus serrulata*). The main seating area, a meeting place for this large family, is square, marked out by a discreet pattern in the block paving. The hard landscaping is an understated combination of yellow granite sets, reclaimed sandstone and narrow strips of black and white porcelain stone. It all works very well together, confirming that less really can be more.

Colored ceramic clinker tiles

These are available in a range of colors: slate black and natural white, cobalt blue, moss green and sandstone yellow. Dimensions: 2.4 x 2.4 x 2.1 inches (6 x 6 x 5.4 cm) or 2 x 2 inches (5 x 5 cm), compatible with regular clinker tile formats. Their advantage is that they can be fitted into water-bound surfaces. Dormann & Wassermann, Schulberg 17, 96482 Ahorn-Wohlbach, Germany. Tel +95 65 7230, www.keramik-werkstatt.de.

Garden design	Droll & Lauenstein, Coburg, Ger
Location	Coburg, Ger

A youthful design

The most attractive gardens tend to be the ones which have developed naturally and matured over the years. Planning a garden like this requires a strong design concept, forward vision, and clients and owners who are prepared to invest in the long-term. This is not an attitude we often see today. We are all more impatient these days, and the new generation of landscape architects tends to favor designs which are appealing, but which have an immediate impact. Why wait, when you can enjoy the finished product straightaway? Clients have also begun to think like this, and there is increasing demand for a complete finished garden package. Turf for the lawn is now almost a basic requirement.

The show garden

The brief was to design a garden for a flower show in London, so in this case, it was essential for the garden to have a full and immediate impact. In the second half of May, the "Chelsea effect" makes it possible to design and build a fantastically realistic garden in only 4 or 5 days, based around any theme, be it historical, rural or even surreal. Every garden has to be 100% realistic, as competition is fierce and, in some cases, the budget seems to be unlimited.

The garden

We must not forget that any design destined to display a wholly original concept to the public for a few short days involves more than just a little showmanship. Above all, this garden is made to appeal to those who like clear, graphic lines. Perhaps it also signals the end of a trend towards naturalistic, timeless and elegant designs. At first glance, this looks like a snippet of checkerboard, grass green squares alternating with the beige. Instead of pawns, bishops and kings we find stone pyramids and hemispheres. A restrained palette of colors is restful on the eye: the green of the box bushes and lawn highlighted by sandstone, gravel and polished sandstone slabs on the bench and tabletop is sufficient. The cubes also fit into this color scheme; only a few herbaceous plants dare to bend the rules a little. It is exactly this precision, painstakingly maintained, that breathes life into the garden. The lawn needs to be mowed and rolled once or twice a week to keep it as neat as a bowling green. The overall charm would soon be lost if the grass were allowed to flower and spread unchecked over the pristine paving stones, or if the box bushes were not clipped three times per season – by hand, of course. An electric hedge-trimmer could never perform the job with such precision.

Garden design   Graduates of the Pickard School of Garden Design, London, GB

Location   Chelsea Flower Show, London, GB

Sandstone and green paint a refreshing picture
and form a welcome addition to any garden.
This design would be equally at home in a small
courtyard, or as a discrete section of a much
larger garden.

The need for space

There is not much here, but it is enough. A new sign of our times is this yearning to flee our overcrowded, extravagant lives, and to find some respite from sensory overload. We need to explore moderation. Pared down architecture, clarity and simplicity of design gave rise to the aphorism "less is more", attributed to Mies van der Rohe (architect, 1886–1969). The need for space, pure and simple, is currently in vogue. Clear lines, simple shapes, geometric designs; nothing too complicated, no glaring colors; simple solutions, solitary pieces of furniture. One eye-catching detail in the garden is enough. A good design example to follow is the 15th century Japanese rock garden, constructed almost entirely from stone, including waterways represented by gravel, and a few specially selected plants.

The garden

Arizona experiences extremes of climate to which all construction must adapt. Houses are plainly built, with few windows and flat roofs – at best an unappealing style from the outside, but essential for keeping the intense temperatures down. Landscaping has to follow the dictates of nature. The ground is left plain, covered with the standard local stone chippings to reflect the heat. Planting is reduced to a minimum. A group of yuccas (*Yucca rostrata*) of various ages and sizes take over where temperate gardens would normally display specimen trees. A solitary African tender fountain grass (*Pennisetum setaceum*) lurks bashfully in the background. Our own gardens, or the spaces outside our offices, may well take on a similar design in anticipation of mild winters in years to come, if we can content ourselves with a minimalist design and severe restrictions on our choice of planting. Less is more. Mostly.

Instead of local stone chippings from Arizona …

… we could use gravel. Sourced from rivers, glaciers, the Baltic Sea or made from quartz, gravel is available in a range of colors. Rough-edged chippings of local European stones, such as basalt or granite, are currently in vogue. Larger areas may require larger stones, up to about 2½ inches in diameter (60 mm). Crushed glass, usually available in blue or bottle green, is also worth considering.

Instead of a yucca …

… another evergreen could take center stage: maybe a mountain pine (*Pinus mugo*) or holly (*Ilex crenata*), clipped into a bonsai shape, or even a standard wisteria, with a tall, straight trunk. A sizeable olive tree, with its distinctive bark formations, would look perfect in a warm, vine-growing area, or indeed anywhere, as long as winter protection could be provided. Bamboo is also worth trying, depending on the available space; a *Fargesia* for example, or the much larger *Phyllostachys*. For more information about bamboo, visit www.bambus-info.de.

But is it art?

This is often our first reaction when we come across an unusual design solution. Is it just a stopgap, or is it art? Is it deliberate, or just coincidence? It is not easy to find good solutions for small, forgettable spaces such as traffic islands, where both the budget and the motivation to produce a good design are limited. Before the days of crushed glass mulch and other such attractive materials, the usual scheme included an arrangement of rocks, perhaps a bearberry cotoneaster (*Cotoneaster dammeri* 'Skogholm', now known as *Cotoneaster × suecicus* 'Skogholm'). Although prized for their ground-covering capability, the plants did not grow well, and soon the long, leggy twigs clumped together in hummocks of green. Some traces of these are still around today. Luckily, we have developed a range of alternatives which are not just stopgap solutions, as we can see here.

The concept

The idea here is to add value. The space is small enough that every inch can be filled, and the materials shown off to their best advantage. From a distance, the eye is automatically drawn towards the bright blue of the glass chippings; from far away, they give the illusion of water, although such a small expanse of water would soon be smothered by algae. The illusion is perfect. The pool is made of glass, a material which can be picked up and held. As the glass has been crushed, there is no danger of it shattering. The green spheres are planted following the exact lines of the natural stone wall we see in the background. All the box spheres are identical, and contrast beautifully with the deep blue glass. The low maintenance requirements of the mulch compensate for the relatively high-maintenance spheres.

Hints and tips

Precision planting makes this feature slightly complicated to install. It is advisable to request a sample of glass, as colors can vary. The bed for the crushed glass needs to be about 4 inches (10 cm) deep and lined with a membrane. Box does not like to be planted too deeply, so it is best to carry out the planting first, then dig the bed for the blue glass chippings. Glass chipping ponds can be ordered from: Recycling Otto A. Müller, Hamburg, www.oam.de.

Warning! New strain of fungal disease threatens plants

A new strain of fungal disease is affecting box, causing discoloration or even causing the foliage to die back completely. Edging box (*Buxus sempervirens*) is the variety most commonly affected. Currently, the only method of control is rigorous plant hygiene. Check new plants thoroughly for falling or discolored leaves (black or brown). Do not plant too densely, and water at the base. The fungus thrives in damp conditions. Remove and dispose of the affected parts immediately, but do not compost.

Garden design   Murdoch Wickham, Sevenoaks, GB

Location   London, GB

Less is not only more; it is easier on the eye. If the green box leaves and the chips of blue glass are the same size, the styling is perfect.

A modern seascape

The "genius loci" (the protective spirit of a place) is a fundamental concept to consider when designing a garden or planning building work. It refers to the "feel" of a place, the atmosphere it radiates. It should ideally be a source of positive energy, which is why it is advisable to try to form an idea of the atmosphere of your chosen location before making a purchase. Have a look at the surrounding land and buildings, and request information about any planned building developments. Whether you choose a coastal location, forest, countryside or city suburbs is essentially a matter of personal preference. It is important to consider your own feelings, or it will be difficult to settle. This particular plot brooks little discussion. It is a seaside location with all that that entails. You either love it or you hate it.

The garden

This garden is in Bexhill, in the south of England. The view of the English Channel is exactly what the owners love about it. A formal garden was not strictly necessary, as a view of the sometimes stormy sea was enough in itself, but some form of access was needed. The entrance was embellished to make it more inviting. The problem was that any planting or landscaping is constantly battered by sea winds carrying salt spray and fine sand. Intense sunlight can be another problem. Stephen Woodhams, who was selected to do the planning, decided that symmetry should be the key. He designed a path of varying widths leading from the house to the beach, ending with five steps directly down onto the sand. Clinkers were the material of choice; they sit well in a costal landscape.

They dry quickly and are relatively resistant to the growth of algae. Sandstone walls, some 20 inches (50 cm) high flank the path, providing a degree of wind protection for the narrow planting beds. Low woven willow fences encase stone beds laid out with pebbles found on the beach. The line of vision is interrupted in the middle as the paved area gives way to two lawns. On this spot, Woodhams has placed a stone urn, filled with stone spheres. The effect is inviting, and almost maintenance-free.

Plants for coastal areas

The coastal climate is mild but demanding. Not many plants can thrive in the constant, salt-laden breezes. Sea buckthorn (*Hippophae rhamnoides*), holly oak (*Quercus ilex*) and laurestine (*Viburnum tinus*) act as windbreaks to protect other species. Lavender and box do well in containers, while these perennials can be planted out: beard tongue (*Penstemon*), bergenia, sagebrush (*Artemisia*), stonecrop (*Sedum*) and straw flower (*Helichrysum*). Further back, the willow fence protects rows of cotton lavender (*Santolina*). It is also well worth trying hedgehog rose (*Rosa rugosa*) and scotch briar (*Rosa pimpinellifolia*).

Garden design   Stephen Woodhams, London, GB

Location   Bexhill, GB

Nature in detail

Inspiration is the key to good design. It can be triggered in any number of ways, and come from any number of sources, not least the brief, the client's wishes, the position of the land and its environment. Creativity is obviously influenced in no small way by current trends in garden design and by classical and modern architecture, but fine art, product design, fashion, the effect of show gardens and far eastern temple gardens all have a part to play. Despite all this input, all these possibilities, the final decision rests with the designer. It takes courage and personal conviction to create something totally different, but it is usually worth taking the risk.

here and there by erratic rocks, now overgrown with moss and algae. It is a modern garden, full of inspiration, representing a beautiful landscape and capturing the imagination of the observer.

The garden

Minimalism meets Japanese garden design. To an esthete, a plethora of different flowers and colors just seems wasteful. The limited range of materials and the restrained design we see here is refreshing. Christian Fournet's show garden depicts a fantasy scene, drawing together elements of the Scottish Highlands, a glacial landscape and the Japanese Islands. The choice of materials is restrained, the materials themselves unusual. Small slabs of sandstone, destined otherwise for the scrap-heap, take center stage, loosely layered up in a flowing fish-scale pattern. The slabs are not uniform; the overall effect is that of a glacial stream winding its way down the mountain into the valley. The green hillocks are covered with pillows of pearlwort. Sparkling white marble chippings symbolize the sea, punctuated

More moss!

Heath pearlwort and reindeer moss are evergreen plants native to Europe and the USA. They grow on stones, and are frequently found in damp forest location. They favor peat-rich soils. Moss is readily available to buy; for retail purposes it is normally grown on a plantation and raised specifically for garden use. Pearlwort is actually a member of the carnation family, but is similar to moss. Most similar of all is procumbent pearlwort (*Sagina procumbens*), a plant which quickly grows to cover large areas. It is often planted between widely-spaced natural paving. Procumbent pearlwort bears lots of tiny white flowers in May and June. It is equally at home in sunshine and shade, but prefers damp conditions. It can also be raised from seed.

Garden design   Christian Fournet, Courbevoie, F

Location   Saint Jean de Beauregard, F

Floating in the air

A garden should be uplifting, and should buoy up our mood. As long as we are not too attached to dark green yew hedging or a stolid rustic look (designs which have been mostly consigned to the past anyway) we can achieve the required lightness by combining a number of components. Paving can be replaced with gravel walkways; and hard surfaces should be kept to a minimum; dark stone (basalt for example looks heavier and can be replaced with light-colored stone e.g. sandstone). Wooden surfaces on paths and patios look friendly and inviting, although decking is not as popular now as it was. The background murmur of fountains and other water features can enhance the atmosphere, even though these have fallen out of favor with the radical garden esthete. Understandably so, really; water features have spent decades at the top of everybody's list of must-haves. Their place has been taken by objets d'art, light features and glass pyramids. You could consider taking up a new hobby: plant collecting is all the rage, and can be fun. All your new acquisitions would breathe new life into a tired garden.

The concept

This slightly sloping plot needs careful planting to keep it lively, and to make the most of its unusual depth. There is no need for a seating area or pergola to draw the visitor in; a path leading all the way through the delightfully planted beds does this admirably. Such was the idea behind the floating steps, which look so comfortable you want to sink down into them. Their dimensions are 36 x 18 inches (90 x 45 cm). The leading edge is only 2½ inches deep (6 cm), although the riser measures almost 6 inches (14 cm), which gives the impression of 'floating steps'. The effect is highlighted by the lovingly planted layer of baby's tears (*Soleirolia soleirolii*) in between. The steps are set into a concrete foundation, and their edges disappear into the beds where they mingle with feather grass (*Stipa tenuissima*), the scented rose 'Roseraie de l'Hay' and salvia 'May Night'. As an alternative, the 'U' shaped prefabricated 'Karlsruhe Garden Stone' could be used for the steps: 16 x 16 x 4/2½ inches (40 x 40 x 10/6 cm), of the type popular in the 70s and 80s for use in walls and steps. When positioned with its 'U' shaped opening to the front, a similar effect can be achieved to that in the photograph.

Collecting plants: a fascinating new trend

- Hostas: a vast range of leaf shapes, colors and even flowers make these highly collectable.
- Ornamental Onion (*Allium*): a good dozen or more varieties to choose from. Remember that bulbs need to be planted in fall for early summer flowering. Order in summer to be sure of your chosen variety.
- Cranesbill (*Geranium*): a wide-ranging category which includes all sizes of plants. The new 'Jolly Bee' grows to a good height and bears blue flowers until the first frosts.
- Bishop's Hat (*Epimedium*) is coming back into fashion fast.

Garden design   Andy Sturgeon, Brighton, GB

Location   London, GB

Steps help us glide through this space – and also
invite us to sit down. They do not lead to front
door or garden gate; their sole purpose is to
enhance our enjoyment of the garden.

Short and to the point

Modern gardens can sometimes look a little bizarre, which is not a bad thing, bearing in mind that the aim of the design is often to modernize and change. The initial effect can be bewildering, too far removed from everyday life. It is worth making the effort to look a bit more closely.

The garden

In a normal setting, this design would take some getting used to. Would anyone be happy to approach this wooden bench and sit down on it? But it makes the perfect show garden, demonstrating just how effective the use of a limited number of materials can be. "Sharp and spiky" is the leitmotif, referring to more than just the mescal and club palms (*Cordyline*) in the foreground. One has found its way into the beach pebbles, which are the rather lovely stones with white markings to the right and left. Between them is a triangle built up of black slate chips, positioned to stand on end. It is unusual to use this as ground cover; it is expensive, and time-consuming to lay. An astonishing amount of material is used. All the gaps would have to be filled before this surface could be walked on, but then it would lose its pleasing, open look (beach pebbles and slate: NVN Natursteinvertrieb Nord in Rellingen, www.nvn.de).

Garden design	Nick Allen, Brighton, GB
Location	Hampton Court Palace, GB

110

Step for step

Changes in level can brighten up any garden. Whether you need to define naturally existing slopes and steps, or to create new ones, the effect is the same; to draw the eye away from a plain, flat expanse, and instead stimulate the observer with all kinds of vertical surfaces. Plants, trees and shrubs can add as much vertical interest as the hard edges of concrete, stone or steel. For the best effect, the garden should slope upwards away from the house, as this can make it look bigger or longer than it actually is.

The garden

When analyzed in detail, the features that make this garden feel so exciting are hardly earth-shattering: the upward slope is defined by three flat stone steps leading towards the back of the garden. They are a prominent feature, not a necessary evil, or even a nuisance, but positively highlighted. Each step is sustained throughout the garden, in the lawn, the water and the herbaceous border. An added design feature is the way in which the steps work as a weir in the water; the water trickles away at its own leisurely pace. Triangular beds have been set in to the corners of the steps, and are planted with trumpet lilies. To the left of the canal, three sections of lawn are separated by three slanting steps, and taper off towards the back of the garden. The middle lawn features a quirky and imaginative stone and glass sculpture (Lucien Simon, from the Hanna Peschar Sculpture Garden), adjoining a mixed border of shrubs and perennials. The charm of this show garden lies not only in the modern materials and the relaxed design, but also in the contrast of steel and glass with the gentle green of the grass and the lavish planting.

The plants

On the right we can see a Japanese dogwood (*Cornus kousa*) in full bloom. Small fruits, rather like raspberries, will form in fall. Next to it is a pretty variety of grass, the tufted sedge (*Carex elata* 'Aurea'). Trumpet lilies (*Zantedeschia aethiopica*) thrive in the marsh bed in the water. Their brilliant white flowers are at their peak in spring and early summer. If the rhizomes are overwintered in a frost free environment, the flowers can bloom year after year. The border behind the glass and steel sculpture is a colorful mix of herbaceous perennials and shrubs, starting with the perfect companion for the sculpture: a palm lily (*Yucca gloriosa*). Further on, we see angelica, wisteria, coleus, bugloss, peonies, roses, viburnum and daylilies.

Garden design   Michael Balston, Patney, GB

Location   Chelsea Flower Show, London, GB

Step by step

It is not easy to find a stylish solution for a garden with marked changes in level. Not only is the financial outlay quite considerable, but it can be difficult to adapt to the feel of the garden and to the prevailing conditions. In one garden, a flight of stairs might look inviting, majestic and grand, but in another, it can make the space seem small and oppressive, quite literally a stumbling block. At the design stage, it is important to remember that steps can naturally affect the appearance and feel of a garden. They need to be safe and easy to climb. It takes on average seven times as much energy to climb a flight of stairs as it does to cover the same distance on the flat. It needs to be worth the effort.

The garden

There is a staggering 20 ft (6 m) difference between street level and the front door of this family home. The stairs leading up to it have to be really inviting and easy to climb, or despair would set in! The design focuses on off-center steps of varying lengths, with slightly larger landing areas in between, where you can catch your breath. The attractively structured Würzburg shell limestone has been used for these steps. At 47 inches in width (1.2 m) the blocks measure approx. 7 x 14 inches (18 x 35 cm). In situ, however, the tread is reduced to 12 inches (30 cm). The conditions did not allow for a uniform pattern of regular steps; the design had to be tailor-made to conform to the natural slope. In spring, 'White Dream' tulips add brightness, against a foil of green Japanese sedge (*Carex morrowii* 'Variegata'), and hostas (*Hosta tardiana*

'Halcyon'), reaching for the sun with their first leaves. A number of yew hedges (*Taxus baccata*) serve to emphasize the clean lines. As this is a private garden, the owners decided against a handrail, giving a more elegant effect.

The correct measurements

Designing a flight of stairs is not just about climbing from A to B as quickly as possible; style and comfort are also of the utmost importance. The dimensions of an individual step are based on an average value of 24–25 inches, giving an average of 24½ (61–64 cm, averaging at around 63 cm). To construct a step requiring low energy input, we use the formula: 2 x rise + 1 tread = 25 inches (63 cm). Thus most steps measure around 6 x 13 inches (15 x 33 cm), as this corresponds to 2 x 6 inches + 13 = 25 (2 x 15 cm + 33 cm = 63 cm). Because of its steep slope, the garden in the photograph required slightly higher risers of 7 inches. Where steps have a riser of less than 5½ inches (14 cm) or over 7½ inches (20 cm), the risk of stumbling is higher. A step dimension of 6½ x 12 inches (16 x 30 cm) would be practical for an outdoor flight in a high traffic area. The steps should not exceed 1–2%, which must be factored into the design.

Garden design and construction   Thomas Heumann, Weinstadt, Ger

Location   Stuttgart, Ger

Symmetry: a winning design

Opinions are divided about geometrical garden design. If the design only consists of geometrical lines, sharp angles and perfect shapes, the effect can be too stark, too "architectural". Symmetry is a different matter, and brings a relaxed neatness into the design. The line of symmetry is most often also the line of vision.

The concept

Symmetry is a major feature in the exterior design of this house. Two high windows and a double door open on to the garden, and the dormer window is centrally located. The clean lines are echoed by the patio, which is used as an extension to the living room, weather permitting. In other situations, it would have been more practical to build the patio at the side of the house, leaving an uninterrupted view, but in this case it was sited at the rear, in the interests of good balance. The kitchen leads off to the right, complete with its own terrace and herb garden.

The garden

The patio is centrally positioned in relation to the living room, but extends out to the side on the left, to do justice to a stone water feature and to provide easier access to the sunny seating area and the front garden. The area measures some 18 x 18 ft (5.5 m x 5.5 m) and is paved with pale gray Pietra Serena, a renowned Italian sandstone. The seating group (www.garpa.de) is in the center, emphasizing the symmetrical aspect. A 3 ft (1 m) wide gravel path leads off into

the garden from its exact center, flanked by stone edging and narrow borders of blue and white plants. This currently consists of grape hyacinths (*Muscari*) and double tulips, to be followed next season by blue cranesbill (*Geranium* 'Jolly Bee').

New: gravel paths as solid as stone!

Gravel paths can be tiresome. Every time they are used, small pieces of gravel are displaced in every direction, and need to be raked back into place. Recently, a new type of path-building system has been developed, which can provide a solid surface which is permeable to water and air, yet is almost indistinguishable from a "genuine" gravel path. Gravel of the desired color and style is bound with an epoxy resin and laid on the path base. The same process can be used with chippings, and is all carried out on site. A top layer of about 1 inch (25 mm) is all that is needed. Its load-bearing capacity relates directly to the strength of the base on which it is laid. Further information about Terraway® products: Green World Products Deutschland, Gundersweiler, www.terraway.de.

Garden design   Ulrich Timm, Hamburg, Ger

Location   Lübeck, Ger

A favorite spot

It's the little things that make a garden. If the details are right, it feels right. It should always be a joy to go out into the garden, to discover unexpected new details. It was a good few years before the owners of this house hit upon the idea of this highly original seating area.

The garden

Gardens are built on memories. 40 years ago, the grandfather of this family planted a fruit orchard. Most of the trees are gone now, and just an old apple tree remains. The trellis in the background was originally used to start a rambling rose 'Paul's Himalayan Musk' which now measures some 33 ft (10 m), tall and its summer blossoms scramble through the leaves of the tree. The area at the base of the tree soon became a favorite resting-spot for anyone doing yard work. It needed some kind of permanent structure; marble cobbles with clinker bricks fitted in nicely. The owners made their own stone slabs with exposed marble cobbles by lining a form with sand, laying the cobbles on top and pouring on cement. After leaving it to dry for two days, they removed the form, brushed away the sand, and the cobbled pavers were ready to lay. The length of the bricks determined the size of the pavers. They measure 9 x 9 inches (23 cm x 23 cm). The area has a lovely lattice design, dotted with box spheres and container plants. It has become a firm favorite.

Garden design   Ursula Schnitzke-Spijker,
                   Gelnhausen-Hailer, Ger

Location   Gelnhausen-Hailer, Ger

A lesson in classical design

There is a theory that there are relatively few professionally designed gardens in southern Germany, because the natural landscape is already so beautiful and uplifting that adding landscaping to the garden is unnecessary. If the theory is true, then here is the exception to prove the rule. There is room for both, as this garden demonstrates. A fantastic location, magnificent scenery and a beautiful, well thought-out garden design. The comparison may seem a little overblown, but this garden bears striking similarities to the incomparable Villa Gamberaia in Fiesola near Florence, Italy, whose garden is truly magical, with its array of formal pools, box topiary and yew hedging. It reminds one of a stage set, with beautiful views over the rolling hills of Tuscany.

The garden

The fabulous view stretches towards Reutlingen in the low-lying mountains of the Swabian alps. Such a magnificent backdrop merits a carefully designed, sympathetic foreground. It was clear from the start that the garden must complement the house, and that a symmetrical design was called for, with a long, central axis of symmetry. The plot lies on a gentle slope which had to be shored up and leveled, protecting the public highway below. A dark green yew hedge (*Taxus*) and 80 'Annabelle' hydrangeas provided the perfect solution. The owners have privacy, and the plot has a boundary. The garden "stage" is further framed by pyramid hornbeams (*Carpinus betulus* 'Fastigiata'). These are not left to grow unchecked, as they could reach heights of up to 50 ft (15 m), but are trimmed to a size in proportion with the house and garden. Looking out from the terrace, the central axis is made up of a rectangular pool flanked by gravel paths and rows of box spheres. The pool, 25 x 4 x 3 ft (7.5 x 1.2 x 1 m), is edged with custom-made clinker bricks, and breathes life into the scene. Custom-made bricks are also used to pave the terrace. A modest seating area is slotted in opposite the terrace, and blends happily into the picture. In honor of the Italian atmosphere, the paths are laid with marble chippings (grigio perla). At the sides of the garden under the trees, herbaceous borders provide a seamless link to other parts of the garden.

Yew hedging

The owners used common yew (*Taxus baccata*) for the hedging, which needs annual pruning to maintain its density of growth. For best results, the yew should be cut back whilst still young to ensure it keeps its slim silhouette, not more than 20 inches (50 cm) wide. An alternative would be Irish yew (*Taxus baccata* 'Fastigiata') or English yew (*Taxus baccata* 'Overeynderi').

Garden design and construction Hans Fahrion, Notzingen, Ger

Location Thomashardt auf dem Schurwald, Ger

Making your mark

Terraced houses, and houses in newer communities, offer little in the way of space in which to unwind and leave behind the stresses of the day. The smallish area in front of the house becomes nothing more than a repository for bikes and a space for dustbins, while the longer strip of land at the back is no wider than the house itself. Proximity to neighbors with similar interests and family structures should, by rights, lead to friendship. It rarely does, though. Misunderstandings between neighbors are common, and could severely limit the time you want to spend outside. Because you can never tell in advance what your neighbors will be like, it is wise to begin with a design which lets you keep your distance, and every square inch counts.

The garden

This house is in Shepherd's Bush, an expensive and sought-after location in West London. The house itself is big, and the garden, being some 66 x 25 ft (20 x 7.5 m), is also relatively large; certainly big enough for the needs of this family. The plain, simple architecture of the turn-of-the-century townhouse is easy on the eye. The plot is enclosed on three sides by a 6½ ft (2 m) brick wall, built from the same brick as the exterior of the house. It adds privacy, and helps to dampen any noise from neighboring gardens. The clients requested lots of seating and lots of grass to play on; requirements which the designer was easily able to fulfill, while also incorporating the existing fruit trees: two apples and a plum. The structure of the design is strong. The doors of the house open directly onto a paved patio. The off-centre seating area means that access into the garden is unimpeded, and that anyone seated need not be disturbed. Another, larger seating area has been incorporated at the far end of the garden (foreground in the photograph), made from bangkirai hardwood. A pool has been installed here to create an attractive vista from house and terrace, spanned by a wide bridge. Big squashy cushions make this the perfect place to lounge. The bridge leads to the seating area proper. The planting scheme is deliberately sparing, as gardening is not a favorite activity for this family. Even mowing the lawn proved to be hard work, so now a gardening company has been hired to take care of it. The neatly clipped box trees add a great deal to the overall sense of order. They make their mark as evergreens, provide an unobtrusive border for the patio and are a great foil for the fruit trees at their center. Although approximately 3 ft square x 1½ ft high, (1 m² x 0.4 m high), they manage to look like perfect cubes. An evergreen hedge at the end of the garden discreetly screens off part of the pool, lending it an air of mystery.

Garden design Friederike Carstens, London, GB

Location London, GB

Modern *planting*

The charm offensive

All too often, ornamental grasses such as *Miscanthus* are excluded from garden designs, yet grasses can make stunning additions to the garden in fall and winter. They are often ignored, mainly because they take two or three years to reach their peak size, but if we were to allow them that extra bit of growing time, our patience would be rewarded. After a long, hot summer, the grasses form a greater number of plumes than usual, and even the fine-leaved Chinese Silver Grass (*Miscanthus sinensis* 'Gracillimus') may begin to flower. It is worth leaving these reed-like ornamentals unpruned for the season to add winter interest, and then cutting them back the following spring.

The garden

As a rule, ornamental grasses add interest to the border by prolonging the gardening year. Many *Miscanthus* grasses are at their peak in September and October, for example 'Silberfeder' on the left here, which can grow up to 6½ ft (2 m) tall, or the graceful, upright 'Kleine Fontäne'. When early frosts leave their mark overnight, the garden becomes a magical place, made still more enchanting by the sparkling of winter sunshine. An unforgettable picture.

The courtyard at its best

There are hundreds of courtyards just like this one, enclosed by walls of one storey or more, accessible from the building, but which also lead through to the garage or to an access route. This is really the only kind of garden most of us need from day to day. There is a danger that a courtyard can be soulless and lacking in imagination, which is a pity, as it often forms the main view from our living room. It is said that small plots are the most difficult to address. We have no way of knowing how much difficulty was involved in the planning of this design, but we can tell that the result is particularly rewarding.

The concept

The curved lines of the terrace are a feature of the building design. Designer Alexander Koch completed the arc and emphasized it in his design. A step leads down from the terrace to the lawn. The light colored wooden door is made of larch wood, and leads to the garage and carport (clad in dark larch wood).

Materials

The materials define the character of the garden. The decking is made from larch, a native softwood, which must be able to dry quickly if it is to last. This has been achieved by anchoring the supporting posts, which were laid at 28 inch (70 cm) intervals into a concrete base. The boards are spaced approximately ¼ of an inch (5 mm) apart and fixed to the joists with two steel screws. The lavender bed, sunk into a segment of the circle, was once a sandpit. The lawn is curved to echo the lines of the terrace, giving the illusion that this green play area is bigger than it actually is. An attractive array of plants grows as if at random in the adjoining gravel, for example lady's mantle (*Alchemilla*), lavender and cranesbill (*Geranium*). Shrubs of this size, forsythia or mock orange for example, planted in this dark corner would just look forlorn.

The plants

The boundaries of the courtyard are marked by two juneberry trees (*Amelanchier lamarckii*) trained into an umbrella shape. Their canopies develop from several main limbs which blossom in April and May, and bear red fruits in summer. The role of the compact bushes is twofold: on the left they form a hedge to emphasize the curve of the terrace and to enclose it; on the right they underplant the juneberries. The neatly clipped box contrasts beautifully with the spreading perennial planting. The lavender in the sandpit is joined on the terrace by containers of hostas, day lilies (*Hemerocallis*) and roses, all enhancing the atmosphere of the garden. The garden furniture is by Reichenberg-Weiss. The table is set at the same angle as the planks in the decking, and the parasol (Garpa) brings a touch of summer.

Garden design   Koch + Koch Gartenarchitekten, Pähl am Ammersee, Ger

Location   Gauting, Ger

Blooming marvelous

There are always elements in a garden which entice you to come and look more closely. The more colorful flowers are often the ones which reel you in, or perhaps you prefer the heady scent of roses and mock orange (*Philadelphus* 'Dame Blanche'), or the twining goldflame honeysuckle (*Lonicera × heckrottii*). It is not often that the plumes of an ornamental grass have the same effect, not yet, anyway, but they are becoming more popular. They tend to look unpromising, and rely on numbers for effect. This is certainly true of fountain grass, better known now by its botanical name, *Pennisetum compressum*, which is how it is usually listed in plant catalogs, yet close inspection yields unexpected results.

Ornamental grasses

Out of the hundred or so varieties of *Pennisetum*, only a few are suitable for garden cultivation. Most are tropical or subtropical varieties; some *Pennisetums*, *P. villosum* for instance, are annuals used by florists in flower arrangements. The most attractive, and the most suitable for the garden is the oldest cultivar, *Pennisetum alopecuroides* 'Hameln'. This close-up photograph shows its natural beauty. Fluffy tails up to 5 inches (12 cm) long start off greeny-white, fading to a silvery-brown. They look a bit like slim bottle brushes, and in fact were once used for cleaning lamps. This cultivar blooms in summer, earlier than most *Pennisetums*, and lasts well into spring, proving that, to be attractive, flowers do not always have to be colorful. The fountain grass in this garden is complemented by members of the *Poaceae* grass family. They grow alongside silver grass (*Miscanthus*), umbrella bamboo (*Fargesia muriellae*) and hair grass

(*Deschampsia*). The planting is unified, reminiscent of a dune landscape. Care must be taken when arranging plants to ensure that the *Pennisetum compressum* is not dwarfed by its taller relatives. If even more flowers are needed, good complementary planting would include tickseed, (*Coreopsis*) stonecrop (*Sedum*) or traditional roses. These all thrive at the water's edge, in full sunlight and well-drained soil as part of a mixed border. *Pennisetum compressum* looks particularly attractive as a specimen plant on a low stone wall, where its narrow leaves can tumble elegantly down, and its unusual flowers are more easily seen than in a flat border. It is a special feature, and should be treated as such.

Garden design	Brigitte Röde, Köln, Ger
Location	Köln, Ger

Carl Linnaeus – a tribute

It is wholly appropriate that a tribute should be paid to this famous Swedish botanist on the occasion of his tercentenary. We gardeners, especially professional ones, have a lot to thank him for. Carl Linnaeus (1707–1787) invented a classification system for plants, the basis for modern taxonomy, and developed a system for botanical terminology. His theory was that a plant's flower, petals, pistils and stamens determined its class. The divisions and groupings he identified are still in use today. The scientific names for plants classified by Linnaeus are indicated by an additional 'L' after the name.

The garden

The Chelsea Flower Show 2007, at the end of May, was chosen as a suitable platform for this show garden because the English feel a strong affinity for Linnaeus, and because his scientific heritage is housed there. The garden, though a strikingly contemporary design, communicates the Swedes' balanced attitude to both culture and the natural world. The Linnaean plants used are skillfully combined and co-coordinated to give an airy, natural feel. This plot of garden, just a few feet square, symbolizes the landscape and tradition of the Swedish nation. For example, the still, dark body of water is reminiscent of a peaty forest floor; in its center, a spring lies almost hidden under a layer of moss. The water trickles under the paved path, then rushes over a bed of natural pebbles and on out to sea. The damp conditions are perfect for haircap moss (*Polytrichum commune*), one of Linnaeus's favorites, and one that on his journeys through the countryside he used both as a mattress and a cover. Red walls divide the garden into an interesting sequence of rooms. Traditional iron oxide pigment provides their color. Swedish granite has been used to pave the visitor's path in front of the walls and through the garden.

The Plants

Spruce (*Picea omorika*) is a traditional plant, used in the background to enclose the garden. Pine and birch are icons of the landscape of Sweden, the latter easily recognizable by its bright white bark (*Betula utilis* var. *jaquemontii* 'Doorenbos'). Crabapples were grown by Linnaeus in his botanical garden; here we see them as rows of standards, their canopies trained to resemble a roof. Every shrub and perennial planted here was classified by Linnaeus, even the wild strawberry. An attractive snowball tree (*Viburnum opulus* 'Roseum') is right in the field of vision, with evergreen European wild ginger (*Asarum europaeum*) at the water's edge, with Siberian flag iris (*Iris sibirica* 'White Swirl') to its left and foxglove (*Digitalis purpurea* 'Saltwood Summer') behind.

Garden design   Ulf Nordfjell, Stockholm, S
Location   Chelsea Flower Show, London, GB;
currently at the Botanical Garden, Göteborg, S

A pool full of plants

Closely clipped hedging and architectural plants are said to be specialties of Belgian garden design. Even English gardens do not always measure up in this respect. No-one else seems to work so skillfully with box and yew, yet there is an emerging trend to break away from the severity of neatness, and introduce some contrast, but not in the form of loosely planted borders.

The garden

Here we see a combination of three styles. Kitchen garden meets country garden in a contemporary context. The kitchen garden is the most work-intensive and the most intensively used, part of the garden. Soft fruits and vegetables are grown alongside vast swathes of perennials and annuals, which provide cut flowers for the household. The country garden is on the other side of the house. An orchard has been planted to blur the transition from garden to fields and meadows. Last of all there is the modern garden close to the house: a low-maintenance area with clipped box and hornbeam hedges, and two ponds of equal size, sealed with bentonite and uniformly planted with bulrushes. A chestnut wood fence encloses them. What a magnificent, fresh look can be achieved just by using the common bulrush!

Garden design   Luk Logist Avantgarden, Wijnegem, B

Location   Antwerpen, B

A riot of color

Once upon a time, simpler gardens, including kitchen gardens, were really nothing special. The plants were uncomplicated, and they were arranged as pretty little cottage gardens in front of, or behind, the house. In England, the houses of agricultural workers were called cottages. The owners created their gardens depending on their means. Cottage gardens have developed from these humble beginnings into something highly desirable. Simple shrubs, roses, herbaceous perennials and an array of summer flowers combine to produce an effect which can brighten up the grayest day.

The garden

The design for this detail from a show garden aimed to be like a real cottage garden, but the cottage garden concept was not the whole scope of the landscapers' theme. Their inspiration came from the designer William Morris (1834–1896), renowned for his imaginative textile and wallpaper designs. The result is a composition of tried and trusted favorites dancing along a chestnut wood lattice fence. The prairie mallows (*Sidalcea* 'Elsie Heugh') flower all summer long, and are particularly pretty. They can be a little sensitive however, and dislike winter wetness. Next to the mallows, the common teasel (*Dipsacus fullonum*) stands out with its egg-shaped flower heads. The tall stems of South American vervain (*Verbena bonariensis*) stretch up from behind, followed by red beard tongue (*Penstemon*) and Roman chamomile (*Anthemis nobilis*). It takes a great deal of skill to arrange such simple flowers in a way that lifts the spirits all summer long.

Cottage garden flowers to try

Shrubs
- Bluebeard (*Caryopteris × clandonensis*)
- Fragrant viburnum (*Viburnum × carlcephalum*)
- Lilac (*Syringa vulgaris* 'Andenken an Ludwig Späth')
- Hydrangea (*Hydrangea petiolaris* and *Hydrangea paniculata*)
- Juneberry (*Amelanchier lamarckii*)
- Mock orange (*Philadelphus* 'Belle Etoile' and 'Erectus')
- Butterfly bush (*Buddleja*-davidii-hybrids)
- Flowering quince (*Chaenomeles*-hybrids)

Perennials
- Bush mallow (*Lavatera*-olbia-hybrid 'Barnsley', *Lavatera thuringiaca*)
- Catmint (*Nepeta × faassenii* 'Six Hills Giant' and 'Walker's Low')
- Lupin (*Lupinus*-polyphyllus-hybrid 'Edelknabe')
- Shasta daisy (*Chrysanthemum*-maximum-hybrid 'Gruppenstolz')
- Garden peony (*Paeonia officinalis* 'Rosea Plena')
- Perennial phlox (*Phlox*-paniculata-hybrids, such as 'Landhochzeit')

Annuals and biennials
- Sweet Williams, scented pelargoniums, wallflowers, pansies, nasturtiums, poppies, antirrhinums, marigolds and various types of sage

Garden design   Butler Landscapes, Whitchurch, GB
Location   The RHS Flower Show at Tatton Park, GB

Make it interesting!

Garden paths can be boring. They can seem endless, and look both tired and tiring. To relieve the monotony, we can introduce variety and pattern into the paving, vary the widths, and provide erratic blocks and stone seats or benches to sit on.

The garden

Architect Rolf Vierkötter has a substantial network of paths in his garden, yet there was never any doubt that he would plan the design himself. The entrance path, with the help of some discreet, pleasant plants, is there to welcome the visitor. This one is paved with 12 x 12 inch (30 x 30 cm) flagstones, and is wide and welcoming. At a generous six flags wide, it could even be considered over-wide for private use, but to break up the uniformity, a flagstone has been removed at regular intervals, and replaced with 12 x 12 inch (30 x 30 cm) plants of ornamental grass. The architect chose Japanese blood grass (*Imperata cylindrica* 'Rubra', formerly known as 'Red Baron'). This variety has a distinctive color, as its common name suggests: in spring, its yellow-green leaves turn blood-red from the tip downwards. By summer, the whole leaf has turned red and flowery panicles may develop. In contrast to the relaxed, spreading habit of many other grasses, Japanese blood grass grows upright, making it perfect for this position. Unfortunately, it is not frosthardy, so some winter protection is desirable in cooler areas. Low-voltage halogen lighting has been installed behind the path to echo the pattern. Their gently curving aluminum shades make them attractive even during the day. When darkness falls, the light reflects off the inside of the shades and can be trained in any direction, to light up the path, the herbaceous border or to intensify the impact of the blood-red grass.

Plants for effect

- Oatgrass (*Helictotrichon sempervirens*, formerly *Avena*) has striking steely-blue leaves. The flowers can grow up to 4 ft (1.2 m) tall.
- Giant feathergrass (*Stipa gigantea*) also grows to an impressive size. Its wheat-like flowers can reach up to 6 ft (1.8 m).
- Tufted hair grass (*Deschampsia cespitosa* 'Goldschleier') is becoming very popular. Its panicles of yellow flowers in summer are some 2½ ft (80 cm) tall.
- Hostas, with their heart-shaped leaves and pretty, long-stemmed flowers are a good choice for shady spots. *Hosta sieboldii* 'Alba' has pure-white flowers.

Garden design Brigitte Röde, Köln, Ger
Location Solingen, Ger

A feel-good design

It doesn't all have to be all about complexity. With just a few plants, or rather a judicious selection of easy plants, it is possible to design a garden for semi-public use, which stays looking good despite only having the occasional maintenance visit from an experienced gardener. Instead of cool green hedging, we can use a cheerful, colorful plants scheme of trees, shrubs and herbaceous perennials whose growth and development emphasize the changing of the seasons.

The garden

It all looks natural, but coordinating the natural look takes a certain amount of skill. This is almost like a model show garden, squeezed into a 75 x 33 ft (23 x 10 m) plot. The year after the show, the whole garden was transported, slightly enlarged but otherwise with minimal change, to its final destination in London's fashionable Knightsbridge area. Here, it forms part of a prestigious residential development, surrounded by luxurious apartments and penthouses. The design introduces a long, narrow pool at the foot of a granite slab (see photograph, in the background), over which water cascades down in a single, wide band. Broad steps to the left and right of the water feature lead up to the next level, where we find this attractive planted area. The focal point is the three-stemmed birch whose pretty foliage adds spring interest. Birch has a spreading root system which can take up valuable nutrients from the surrounding area. Surprisingly, this is not always a problem. The herbaceous border perennials here cope particularly well, and are thriving. They are catmint (*Nepeta* × *faassenii* 'Walker's Low') together with the almond-leaved leathery

wood-spurge (*Euphorbia amygdaloides* var. *robbiae*), blue bearded iris and a variety of fern. The round flower heads of the lovely allium 'Mount Everest' take center stage in June, when they can reach a diameter of up to 4 inches (10 cm). At around 3 ft (1 m) in height, they seem to hover above the border as if held by some invisible hand. The bed is enclosed by a low growing box hedge punctuated by a natural stone cube. This is an eye-catcher in its own right, but can also be used as seating. The block is made of Portland stone, a natural limestone quarried on the Isle of Portland in England. The block is not just a simple block, however. A narrow gap has been left near the top, into which a ribbon of colored glass has been set. When it catches the light it can cast unexpectedly dramatic patterns. The scheme is undemanding; the plants flower year after year, even the white allium. There is a single shrub here, which also demands its share of attention: the white dogwood (*Cornus alba* 'Argenteomarginata') at the extreme right of the picture. Its creamy-edged leaves serve to highlight the brightness of the surrounding colors in the summer time, while its red bark lifts the color of the winter garden. A word of warning though: dogwood can grow to an astonishing 10 x 10 ft (3 x 3 m) and can encroach on its neighbors, unless pruned annually. The hedges and perennials should also be cut back every year to preserve their shape.

Garden design   Phil Jaffa, Patrick Collins (Scape Design), London, GB
Location   Chelsea Flower Show, London, GB

Modern-day urban gardens can be truly beautiful. A friendly color scheme and low-maintenance planting provide the perfect foil for the stone cube seat.

Good bedfellows

Has this garden been neglected? Surely the tall allium seedheads should have been cut back long before midsummer. The answer is a resounding no! The seedheads are an important component of this contemporary style herbaceous border. The combination of buds and blooms, co-ordinating and contrasting colors, different textures and pods and seedheads is exactly what makes it such a charming sight. It is an indication of the vast choice available nowadays to the keen plantsman. In most cases, flowering bulbs need to be dead-headed when the last petals have fallen, whether lily, daffodil or tulip. Not so the allium. Its unusual seedheads add interest to the border for a number of weeks, until mid July. This is true of most allium varieties, including *Allium christophii, A. giganticum, A.* 'Globemaster', *A. karataviense, A.* 'Purple Sensation' and *A. stipitatum.*

The garden

The plant classification system has an important part to play here. Anja Maubach designs a variety of themed gardens, where frost hardy perennials naturally take center-stage, but other plant families are present in supporting roles. Her plant nursery in Wuppertal-Ronsdorf draws clients from all walks of life; her aim is to demonstrate the range and variety of options and effects one can achieve in an herbaceous border at different times in the gardening year. Her technique is to plant large areas with swathes of perennials in groups according to type, divided into smaller, more manageable sections, as this themed garden shows. In June and July, the border is in full bloom with yellow meadow rue (*Thalictrum*

ssp. *flavum*) and a traditional rose variety, *Rosa alba* 'Mme Plantier', while *Allium* 'Globemaster' seedheads add interest. In the foreground, we can just see a swathe of silver grass (*Miscanthus*). After flowering in May, the floaty, round seed heads provide interesting visual and textural contrasts. Planted in rows, they add a natural flow to the border. In the first spring after planting, their tiny purple flowerlets make a spherical head up to 10 inches (25 cm) across, while in subsequent years, the bulbs send up more shoots, bit the flowerheads are substantially smaller, and look more naturalistic. The seed heads are a fascinating feature, providing visual interest for several more weeks. Each of these remarkable spheres is made up of around 150 tiny star-shaped flowers. Further information about alliums can be found in the section on Anja Maubach's plant nursery in Wuppertal.

Garden design	Anja Maubach, Wuppertal, Ger
Location	Wuppertal-Ronsdorf, Ger

The colors of heaven

Perennials are delightful plants, but they do require care and attention. It takes a certain amount of skill and experience to choose the right combination of flowers and grasses, and to arrange the border in such a way that everything can be seen to its best advantage. Color is not the only consideration; height, growth habit and flowering period are all equally important.

The garden

Here we see a sweeping view of a romantic new planting concept entitled "In the colors of heaven", chosen as the theme for the IGA Rostock Garden Show. There is no comparison between these bold specimens and the gentler, more sensitive flowers of well-known perennials such as baby's breath (*Gypsophila*), bleeding heart (*Dicentra*) or the perennial poppy (*Papaver orientale*). They are all tall and easy to grow. The herbaceous perennials can be planted in the border alongside the grasses in a relatively large space. When the plants have grown and spread, usually after about their second season, weeds simply do not stand a chance. To achieve a worthwhile effect, they need to be planted in groups of ten or twelve, but the size and number can vary substantially, depending on the type of plant and the desired intensity of color. The groupings can be long and narrow or more rounded. The best effect is achieved by repeating the shapes to create a cohesive, yet varied border.

The plants

Right at the front, pride of place is given to a cloud of white coneflowers (*Echinacea purpurea* 'Alba'), with a group of Russian sage (*Perovskia abrotanoides*) behind it, at about 3 ft (1 m) tall. At the back, a swathe of switchgrass (*Panicum virgatum* 'Cloud Nine') promises to grow to double that height. The yellow spikes on the left belong to feather reed grass (*Calamagrostis × acutiflora* 'Karl Foerster'), which will grow to about 5 ft (1.5 m). Silver-leaved willow-pear (*Pyrus salicifolia* 'Pendula') complements the color palette beautifully – we can just see a branch making its way into the photograph on the left hand side – and on the right we see the fresh green shoots of Chinese silver grass (*Miscanthus sinensis* 'Malepartus').

More perennials and grasses

There are many other perennials which flower in the "colors of heaven": Michaelmas daisies (*Aster × frikartii* 'Wunder von Stäfa'), catmint (*Nepeta × faassenii* 'Six Hills Giant'), red bistort (*Persicaria amplexicaule* 'Alba') and salvia (*Salvia nemorosa* 'Steppentraum'). A word of warning here though: salvia is self-seeding, and can be extremely prolific. The same goes for South American vervain (*Verbena bonariensis*), prized for its pretty lavender colored flowers on long stems some 2½–3 ft (80–90 cm) tall; not forgetting Culver's root (*Veronicastrum virginicum* 'Fascination' and 'Lavendelturm') and Chinese fountain grass (*Pennisetum alopecuroides*).

Garden design   Petra Pelz, Magdeburg, Ger
Location   Rostock, Ger

A striking contrast

The subject of conifers, those cone-bearing softwood trees, can cause feelings to run high. Most of us love pines and larches, dark green yew hedges, and especially the remarkable ginkgo tree, but many other varieties, including juniper (*Juniperus*) do not rank among our favorites unless we intend to plant a moorland garden; they do not seem to appeal on any level. To a good professional garden designer, this is a case of throwing down the gauntlet.

The garden

Mark Ashmead's aim was simple: to prove that any sort of conifer can be attractive, even the ones at which we turn up our noses. It is refreshing to see how he has managed to put these common, everyday container plants to such interesting use. All credit goes to his underlying design: he wanted simple, curved shapes to fill the whole space, which is defined by water, wooden terraces and conifers. Curved galvanized steel plates emphasize the sweeping arcs and outline the attractive pattern of the curved beds. Water bubbles up from the center and runs across the various surfaces. Lawns and terraces curve round, alternating with strips of glass pebbles and polished steel plates. Note the misty effect on the right hand side of the photograph: it is achieved using a ceramic membrane technique. Creeping juniper and thuja provide ground-cover. This garden shows conifers in a different light, proving that even they have their bright and cheery side.

Garden design   Mark Ashmead, Chelmsford, GB
Location   The Hampton Court Palace Flower Show, GB

144

New plants with character

Some plants are simply difficult to love, be they house plants or garden shrubs. Mother-in-law's-tongue, for example, attracts few admirers (although this seems to be changing). The garden equivalent would probably be leatherleaf viburnum (*Viburnum rhytidophyllum*). Once upon a time it could be seen in every garden, but now nobody wants it, which is really quite understandable. The leaf surface is wrinkled and hairy, and frosty temperatures make the foliage droop as if in mourning. These viburnums do, however, provide extremely effective screening. Even rhododendrons are often classed as "difficult" plants, since for 11 months of the year, they offer nothing but green.

The garden

There is still hope for the forgotten shrubs. Until recently, nurseries set great store only by those plants which were uniformly green and grew evenly, but fashions change, and we are starting to appreciate different growth habits. Some nurseries now specialize in training trees and woody shrubs into interesting new shapes. Plants like this viburnum can be trained to resemble an umbrella: weaker branches are cut away, and only the strongest are retained. The stems are pruned so that the foliage first begins to sprout at a height of 5–7 ft (1.5–2 m). Suddenly, they are transformed into desirable specimen plants, exuding charm and elegance, and which everybody wants to own. They are at their attractive best in this garden, their striking stems underplanted with cloud-like box hedging. In the foreground, the eye is drawn towards the greater masterwort (*Astrantia major* 'Claret') in an attractive combination with pheasant's tail grass (*Stipa arundinacea*) against a background of red-leaved foxglove beard-tongue (*Penstemon digitalis* 'Huskers Red'). The whole is a splendid blend of traditional shrubs and modern colors.

Trees and shrubs with umbrella-shaped canopies

- Field maple (*Acer campestre*)
- Juneberry (*Amelanchier lamarckii*)
- Common box (*Buxus*)
- Cornel (*Cornus mas*)
- Common hornbeam (*Carpinus betulus*)
- Burning bush (*Euonymus alatus*)
- Crabapple (*Malus* 'Evereste', 'Rudolf')
- Flowering cherry (*Prunus serrulata* 'Kanzan')
- Leatherleaf viburnum (*Viburnum rhytidophyllum*)
- Austrian black pine (*Pinus nigra* ssp. *nigra*)
- Blue Scots pine (*Pinus sylvestris* 'Glauca')
- Canadian hemlock (*Tsuga canadensis*)

Available from Bruns Pflanzen, 26146 Bad Zwischenahn, Germany, www.bruns.de

Garden design Tom Stuart-Smith, London, GB
Location London, GB

Are black plants sexy?

Yes they are, claims Karen Platt, in her book "Black Magic and Purple Passion" (Black Tulip Publishing); no other colors come close. Black plants are the jazz and blues of the plant world. In any case, no-one has yet grown the definitive black rose or tulip, and the search is far from over. A novel by Alexandre Dumas Snr. (1802–1870) about tulip grower Cornelius van Baerle, has a happy ending (at the end of the eighteenth century, a reward of 100,000 Guilders was promised to the first person to grow a black tulip), but in reality, growers are still trying. We have an abiding fascination for dark plants, for shrubs and bulbs with black flowers, and trees with deep red leaves. Their circle of admirers grows with each new discovery.

look black when wet. Compatible plants are alum-root (*Heuchera micrantha* 'Palace Purple') with its reddish-brown leaves, and the feathery foliage of the Japanese maple (*Acer palmatum* 'Dissectum atropurpureum'). A group of hostas (*Hosta sieboldiana* 'Frances Williams') keep them company, along with a very unusual garden plant, Australian tree fern (*Dicksonia antarctica*). This living fossil is fairly hardy, which is one of the reasons for its growing popularity.

The garden

This idyllic scene shows a detail from a much bigger garden, designed for dappled shade. It has a distinctly modern design and planting scheme, concentrating less on the plants and plantsmanship, and more on the architectural aspect of landscape gardening. The effect is dramatic, enhanced by the reflections in the 20 inch (50 cm) wide pool. The stems of black bamboo (*Phyllostachys nigra*) are far more striking as reflections than they are against a background of dark-leaved shrubs. The bamboo is a good 16 feet (5 m) tall, with stiff, upright stems (this is not the case with all bamboo, by any means), and bright green leaves. It is advisable to restrict root growth using a rhizome barrier under the ground, as bamboo is very invasive, and will take over the whole garden within a few years. Dark cobbles from Thailand cover the ground. They

Black, or almost black

- Common columbine (*Aquilegia-vulgaris*-hybrid 'Black Barlow') with its deep purple flowers
- Hollyhock (*Alcea rosa* 'Nigra'), which flowers in its second year
- German iris (*Iris*-barbata-elatior-hybrid 'Night Ruler')
- Virgin's Bower (*Clematis* 'Black Prince'), with deep purple flowers, almost black
- Japanese Shield Fern (*Dryopteris erythrosora*) with its coppery red fronds; evergreen
- Black Dragon (*Ophiopogon planiscapus* 'Nigrescens'), an eggplant-colored "grass"
- Dark-leaved meadow cranesbill (*Geranium pratense* 'New Dimension')
- Tulip 'Queen of the Night', blackish purple, Tulip 'Black Hero' double bloom, deep navy blue

| Garden design | Kate Gould, London, GB |
| Location | London, GB |

Darker hues are absolutely en vogue. Dark gray pebbles and black bamboo stems are here combined with the dark foliage of alumroot (Heuchera).

Strictly for the birds

Gone are the days when every garden center offered a cute little teddy bear for sale as box topiary figures. Or are they? Topiary can certainly be an attractive feature, but it is not to everyone's taste. It also requires regular care and attention. It was the same story with bonsai trees some years ago. Everyone had to have one, but enthusiasm waned when it became clear that the lovely little trees did not stay lovely for long without some intervention. These expensive imports need very specific growing conditions, meticulous daily care and skilful pruning, or they do not thrive. So it is for these green sculptures on the patio. Without regular attention, they would soon lose their shape and grow straggly and unattractive, but the rewards are great for those who look after their birds. One man's (or woman's) hard work is another man's (or woman's) delight.

The garden

Marc de Winter likes to keep his birds on the patio, which looks particularly lovely in early fall. The sculptures are just one aspect in his detailed, meticulously planned garden landscape (see p. 32 and 156). The strong stems on which the birds perch are quite unusual, and are a sure sign that these box trees are advanced in years, as it takes many years to build up such thick wood. The birds are shaped from pot-grown box, which requires proper maintenance. It needs regular watering, and feeding with a proprietary fertilizer. For the first year or two, the wire framework shaping the topiary is very exposed, but patience brings its own rewards, especially for Marc de Winter. He can never have too many birds.

How to create a beautiful bird

- Plant a box, privet or yew, the densest you can find.
- Use a container, or plant out in a border, remembering to create a "saucer" around the plant to hold water.
- Allow about a year before the first pruning.
- Using strong, moderately flexible wire, or strong wire and bamboo, shape your bird (or any other figure of your choosing).
- During growing periods, train the plant by bending into shape and tying the shoots in to the wire frame.
- Side shoots should be trimmed away regularly.
- Container-grown topiary should be protected from frost.

Garden design   Marc De Winter, Bloem Bloem, Halle-Zoersel, B

Location   Halle-Zoersel, B

Like a wild flower meadow

Color has an extraordinary effect on us. It can lift, amaze, enthrall or even irritate. White gardens are still very en vogue even now, 50 years after Vita Sackville-West, in a stroke of genius, had one of her gardens at Sissinghurst Castle turned over to white roses and shrubs. Her idea is often copied, and sometimes even developed further. White can be used to separate other colors, or to make them stand out even more brightly. However, we can sometimes feel compelled to try to make the impossible possible, and we try to find all kinds of black flowers to plant together in one border. (see p. 148). This minimalist approach, although it can be appealing for some, can be almost obsessive. It is far better to stick to a brighter palette of colors, yellow, for example. It may not be everybody's favorite, but it is friendly and inviting.

The garden

Uplifting, bright and full of joy are our first impressions of this wild flower meadow of a garden, planted with yellows, oranges and reds. The gorgeous tall mullein (*Verbascum* 'Cotswold Queen'), with its pretty purple-centered yellow flowers atop stems of up to 4 ft (1.2 m) high, sets the tone, along with the paler yellow *Verbascum* 'Gainsborough'. Both of these flower in July, but regular dead-heading can prolong the flowering period until well into fall. They love a sunny spot, and reach confidently towards the sky in the space of a few short weeks. Foxtail lilies (*Eremurus*) seen here in bud, complement the planting, while a bold group of foxgloves (*Digitalis*) in front of the linden hedge form a backdrop for them. The companion planting, comprising a number of smaller herbaceous plants, is chosen with care to ensure that the taller herbaceous perennials have a firm footing and do not keel over in the wind. It also makes the garden visually more appealing, and more balanced. The relaxed feel of the garden is further enhanced by a loosely spiral set of granite steps which wend their way through the beds to a seating area at the center. They almost seem to be floating. The steps have been laid with small open gaps left between them, which allows for an interesting play of shadows. The planting scheme further softens any harsh lines. The practical aspect of the design is almost incidental. The borders are easily accessed on the right and left of the steps, for purposes of feeding, weeding, cutting, and, when necessary, dividing and transplanting every two or three years. The 12 inch (30 cm) tall avens (*Geum*), which has been somewhat overlooked as a plant recently, is an ideal companion, as is the daylily (*Hemerocallis*), also grateful to be included, and seen here on the inside of the arc. There are countless varieties available in yellow and orange and every shade in between. Gray-leaved perennials make discreet partners; here we see wormwood (*Artemisia*) and the furry silver hedge-nettle (*Stachys*).

Garden design Jane Hudson und Erik De Maeijer, Thompson Landscapes, Goffs Oak, GB

Location Chelsea Flower Show, London, GB

Our old friend, the millstone

Those were the good old days, back in the 70s, when every garden seemed to possess a millstone. These were the genuine article; venerable old granite millstones, pensioned off and then given a new lease of life as a water feature, with the simple addition of a catch pool and a circulating pump. Now once again we are beginning to hear the trickle of water on stone, but this time the millstones are imported from the Far East. They may not have the same charm, but they are cheap, and that is all that seems to matter, and that goes for more than just millstones from China.

The garden

A function of the garden can be to uphold traditions, but that does not mean they have to be carbon copies of the old designs. Once upon a time, millstones were used, worn out and replaced with new ones, so the old ones were incorporated into the garden. Ulf Nordfjell has picked up this concept, and carried it through to a modern garden context. He had a cylinder made from Bolus granite, rather different from the millstones of old. The surface is broached and bush-hammered, is 14 inches (35 cm) thick, and has a recess off-center. It is distinctive, and serves as a reminder of bygone times, inviting the visitor to sit down and enjoy the flower garden. Box spheres make good companions for this heavyweight, but even they cannot take it on alone. As a pair they are stronger, and create an interesting sense of anticipation. They, along with the millstone, creep on to the cobbled path, very much at home in this country garden environment. This is not a direct thoroughfare, more a winding country path whose purpose is not to separate the borders, but to take the edge off any formality, to provide a place from which to tend the planting and, more importantly, from where the visitor can enjoy them at close quarters.

The plants

Common box (*Buxus sempervirens* var. *arborescens*) is present in all its glory, as uniformly shaped spheres which seem to lie on the ground. Between the spheres, the slim stems of the native Swedish Highland pine (*Pinus sylvestris*) are joined by grasses, bulbs and perennials such as giant feather grass (*Stipa gigantea*), whose flowers seem to hover above the garden, or the white orbs of the ornamental onion (*Allium* 'Mont Blanc'), which can grow up to 3 ft (1 m) tall. Then comes the reliable old salvia (*Salvia nemorosa* 'Caradonna'), or, to the left of the granite stone, the little Latin American fleabane (*Erigeron karvinskianus*) which not only flowers continuously until well into the fall, but self-seeds, and conveniently fills any sunny gap.

Garden design   Ulf Nordfjell, Stockholm, S
Location   Chelsea Flower Show, London, GB;
currently at the Botanical Garden, Göteborg, S

Zebra stripes

We humans like to intervene in a plant's natural growth processes. We are forever training, pruning, cutting back and trimming, until the plant looks the way we want it to. Fruit trees are subjected to formative and renewal pruning to ensure a good harvest, but Bonsai trees probably need the most frequent and careful intervention to maintain their miniature perfection. Hedges, on the other hand, only need clipping once or twice a year to keep their shape. A hedge is not always just a hedge, it can produce some dramatic effects.

The garden

Most gardens have a hedge, in most cases separating the garden from the street, and usually to shield it from sight and extraneous noise. This hedge, however, is more of an ensemble than a simple hedge, and it is not strictly needed for any practical purpose, but contributes to the overall esthetic appearance of the space. These are European beeches (*Fagus sylvatica*). The de-limbed trees are planted at the perimeter, at intervals of about 1½ ft (50 cm), dictated by the size of their rootballs. Their white trunks are about 7 ft (2 m) high, at which point the branches begin to grow. A block of young plants, each about 2½ ft (80 cm) are positioned side by side directly in front of the trees, making the hedge a good three feet wide. The tree trunks in the background are further highlighted by planting specimen beeches at 6½ ft (2 m) intervals, whose crowns have been shaped into orbs by Marc de Winter. These are already 3 ft (1 m) across, but it is the color of the trunks rather than the shape which grabs our attention. Painting

the trunks with whitewash fulfills two design criteria in one. Firstly, unprotected beech trees, like fruit trees, are susceptible to sunburn, and secondly, it looks good from an artistic point of view. The knotty trunks catch our eye precisely because of their color, and become a real focal point.

In fashion again: white tree trunks

Whitewashing the trunks and lower branches of fruit trees is a long-established technique which is coming back into fashion for practical and esthetic purposes. The light color reflects the sun better than dark-colored bark. It protects the trees from frost damage, which can introduce pests and diseases. Whitewashed bark retains its elasticity and inhibits the growth of moss. (Schacht's "White Tree Paint" is a weatherproof combination of sea minerals, trace elements and silicic acid). It is best applied between November and March. Before application, remove any moss and lichen, which is commonly found of the trunks of trees growing in dense shade.

Garden design	Marc De Winter, Bloem Bloem, Halle-Zoersel, B
Location	Halle-Zoersel, B

An extended family

Evergreen box has an important role to play in many gardens, as a hedge, a sphere, a pyramid, or in a group. Maintenance is not difficult, and the shrub can tolerate some very close clipping. It never vies for center stage, but carries on looking attractive long after its perennial and deciduous companions have lost their appeal.

The garden

Hamburg boasts a good number of gardens like this one, backing on to the water, and this is certainly not the first design this plot has ever seen. This particular garden has been landscaped before. For years, the planting scheme had been lavish and luxuriant. White shrub roses 'Schneewittchen' bloomed alongside various other herbaceous perennials, bulbs and the *Rhododendron* 'Cunningham's White', all in white, against a background of yew, and enclosed by a box hedge. Then the client decided it was time for a change, and opted for minimalism. The roses were all given away, as were the perennials. Only the rhododendron remained. Before the box bushes, too, could be given away, they were gathered together and planted as a family group. The evergreen enclosure was retained as a reminder of the old flowerbed. The only white summer flowers present now are *Allium* 'Mont Blanc' and African lilies (*Agapanthus*). The shape of their heads echoes the spheres of box. A single white accent-piece adorns the seating group at the water's edge: a 7 ft (2.15 m) white standard lamp by Metalarte.

Garden design   Ulrich Timm Grünplanung, Hamburg, Ger

Location   Hamburg, Ger

Seeking sanctuary

For many of us, our dream garden would be our refuge, a protected place where we would feel safe and where we could spend time undisturbed with those dearest to us. It takes expertise and a sensitive touch to conjure up this sort of atmosphere. Garden owners' expectations are all different. Some like to surround themselves with a wealth of plants and objects, while others prefer a minimalist approach. Planting and color also come down to personal choice. The garden is often influenced by its neighbors, particularly by tall, established trees. Trees are important, not only for the shade they provide, but under the right circumstances, they can also give a garden a cozy, enclosed feel.

The reflections merit a second glance. They are distorted by the water, but completely unique.

The garden

An atmosphere of well-being is paramount in this garden. Rather than feeling elitist, however, it has the comfort of familiarity and an instinctive appeal. A group of New Zealand sedges (*Carex*) skillfully hide the rapidly yellowing leaves of the ornamental onion (*Allium* 'Purple Sensation'). Even the blood-red Japanese barberry (*Berberis thunbergii* 'Bagatelle') seems happy in its role of thorny edging plant. An eminently suitable companion is the orange triumph tulip 'Prinses Irene'. Gray cushions of cotton lavender (*Santolina chamaecyparissus*) provide an elegant foil, punctuated at intervals with foxgloves (*Digitalis*). Watching over them all is a row of pyramid hornbeams (*Carpinus betulus* 'Fastigiata'), whose smooth trunks add height to the design and echo the vertical lines of the wall, as does the strikingly unusual water-feature: a polished stainless steel wall of trickling water with a pale blue eye.

Standard trees and shrubs

- Japanese angelica tree (*Aralia elata*) is notable for its unusual prickly trunk and elongated feathery leaves, up to 28 inches (70 cm) long.
- Cornelian cherry (*Cornus mas*), small yellow flowers in March; red fruits.
- Globe head Norway maple (*Acer platanoides* 'Globosum') a well-known globe-headed variety, whose crown can reach up to 20 feet (6 m) across when fully grown. This should be taken into account when planting, or the garden will end up feeling small and shady.
- Black locust (*Robinia pseudoacacia* 'Umbraculifera') grows up to 13 ft (4 m) tall, and will tolerate radical pruning, but not too deep into the old wood.
- Crimson Midland hawthorn (*Crataegus laevigata* 'Paul Scarlet') has a rounded canopy with long, sharp thorns, laden with double crimson blooms.
- Crab apple (*Malus* 'Evereste') grows in the shape of a wide-based pyramid and has pink-speckled white flowers, which develop into red-flushed fruits.

Garden design   Stephen Woodhams, London, GB
Location   Chelsea Flower Show, London, GB

Willow pattern

Although willow is a frail material, it is prevalent, as it has other properties which make it popular. There are various types of willow available to work with, but the most common is osier (*Salix viminalis*). It thrives in damp conditions or at the water's edge, and is usually harvested in winter. This helps to maintain the cultivated areas, and also provides material for basket weaving, erosion control on slopes and stream banks and for living fences and even buildings. The International Garden Show IGA in Rostock, Germany was home to a 50 ft (15 m) willow cathedral in 2003.

The fence

Here is a common problem. For safety reasons, the driveway to the garage needs to be fenced off. A bed of shrubs is not quite enough, and will not suit the front garden. A hedge would look too heavy. These clients were keen to find a natural solution; a transparent willow fence seemed to be the perfect answer. The fence was woven from a mixture of living willow rods and thinner material which will not sprout. The stronger rods were driven into the ground to a depth of some 12 inches (30 cm), and the soil was improved with the addition of humus. The thinner whips were then woven across, leaving a gap between each group. In the first few weeks, the fence needs copious watering to encourage the vertical rods to take root, for enhanced stability, after which the structure becomes relatively low-maintenance. The new shoots are cut back once a year (when the moon is full) to keep the fence looking light,

and to stop the interlaced whips from becoming too wide. It also allows this sun-loving South American vervain (*Verbena bonariensis*) to flourish and to display its flowery tufts year after year.

More about willow

Willow is best harvested during its dormant period in winter. The cuttings should be kept moist in a dark, airy place, and not permitted to dry out. Between February and April is the best time for planting, although the period from June to November is also acceptable, depending on the weather. Thin whips are the most suitable for weaving, although specialist weavers have developed techniques for working with thicker stems (www.flechtwerk-hamburg.de). Acacia wood is often used for support in these cases. A willow fence can last ten years or more. They can take a huge range of forms and structures. The vertical rods will keep sprouting new green shoots, as long as they are driven at least 12 inches (30 cm) into the ground. Stability is improved if they are set at an angle. They can be tied together wherever two branches cross.

Garden design	Ulrich Timm, Hamburg, Ger
Construction	W. Bielfeldt (Steffen Kron), Börnsen, Ger
Location	Hamburg, Ger

In the urban jungle

We have all seen gardens that have become a tangle of lilac and elderberry bushes growing out of control, because they have been left to themselves. They clamber over walls and open spaces, and bathe what used to be a sunny garden in deep shadow. Acers, chestnuts, acacias and other trees also like to spread themselves out if left to grow unchecked. This is what we tend to mean by a jungle of a garden. But the garden can also be jungle-like by design, in which case the atmosphere is altogether more exotic.

The garden

Overgrown gardens and aging trees hiding behind high walls are not uncommon in an urban setting. They are often neglected because nothing worthwhile in the way of trees or flowers can flourish in these conditions, but introduce a touch of the exotic, and the atmosphere can change completely. Such was the trigger for designer Phillippa Probert, whose aim was to move away from the elegant, feel-good style of the city, veering rather towards the wild, uncontrolled jungle feel. She introduced a lovely pale-blue wall as a backdrop, which can be seen from between the plants like a distant sea. Not only are palm trees used to evoke the beautiful side of the jungle landscape, but also tree ferns (*Dicksonia antarctica*) of varying heights. This is a shade-loving variety native to temperate rainforests, and also suitable for our climate.

The exotic jungle species are complemented by native ferns and mosses, and also by bellflowers (*Campanula*) and the pretty false goat's beard (*Astilbe arendsii*

'White Gloria'). They spill out over the gravel paths and natural looking paving stones, which are in fact made from recycled granite reinforced with glass fiber. The center of attention, though, has to be the red glass building (Bartholomew Contemporary) which, at 7½ x 7½ ft (2.3 x 2.3 m), is big enough to flee to when we need to escape. Or it could be the workplace of the future, with fast internet access plus views of an enchanted dreamscape, somewhere between paradise and reality.

Tree ferns

Tree ferns have been around since the Paleozoic era, about 400 million years ago. Today they are found in tropical or subtropical rainforests, especially in Australia and New Zealand and neighboring countries. The *Dicksonia antarctica* variety is relatively hardy, and can even tolerate a few degrees of frost. The trunk and root area should be protected with some form of natural horticultural fleece before the onset of winter. The long fronds, up to 7 ft (2 m), can perish in extremes of cold, but will grow back when the weather improves. Spring is the best time for planting. Available from: www.baldur-garten.de, www.tropengarten.de.

| *Garden design* | Phillippa Probert, Wirral, GB |
| *Location* | Tatton Hall, Knutsford, GB |

Modern *extras*

A pool within a pool

We have a long tradition of including pools in our parks and gardens. They cut an imposing figure in a formal Baroque garden, often with the addition of an impressive fountain. Stately homes and palace gardens give them pride of place on the main avenue, obliging visitors to take a more circuitous route. Plants and fish stock are usually quite spare. The garden pool tradition still endures today, but is reduced to today's dimensions, and instead of a grand sandstone border, we tend to prefer something a little more discreet.

The design

This is a very innovative show garden. It incorporates a large pond in a rather similar way to an old palace garden, but within a modern context. The pond had to be circular (well, almost) and is about 16½ ft (5 m) in diameter. It is shallow enough to reveal its base of basalt chippings. The shape is not a perfect circle, however; a small bay area projects out at one point. In the center are two concentric smaller pools, adding further interest to the picture in an understated way. A striking effect for a relatively low-maintenance installation.

Garden design   Stephen Morgan, Patricia Stainton, Frome, GB

Location   Westonbirt, GB

A charming old craft revisited

A few years ago, it was almost unthinkable that stonemasonry would enjoy such a revival. Dry stone walls and stone gardens had had their day, and only Friesian dry stone walls, traditionally a feature of Northern Germany, were built outside their home environment, but somehow even they looked out of place. Now, though, dry stone walling has found its niche again, and is even used to construct objets d'art. If the workmanship is good, the finished wall does not need a barrage of plants to conceal it.

The garden

It is marvelous to see how few materials are required to create such a cheerful atmosphere in this garden. The focal point, shifted slightly off-center, is this unusual stone sphere, but without the usual bubbling water. It took 22 layers of Yorkshire sandstone to build this 2½ ft (70 cm) diameter sphere. Each individual layer consists of several slabs, rounded at the perimeter, and fitted together like slices of cake. Each one is unique; this is craftsmanship indeed. Andrew Loudon, from the county of Cumbria in England, is a true expert in this field, and here is a prime example of the quality of his dry-stone work. It is clear that the stone is individually shaped by hand rather than coming off a production line, and it does not need the addition of trickling water to add interest. The work took Andrew Loudon three days to complete. A summery planting scheme, relaxed yet cheerful, makes the perfect foil.

The colors of summer

This modern perennial planting scheme is cheerful and lively, quite rural, not unlike a cottage garden. Grasses add a good finishing touch. These are faithful tried and trusted plants. The dazzling red flowers belong to the avens (*Geum coccineum*), a clump-forming perennial with evergreen foliage which is hidden here by feather grass (*Stipa tenuissima*). Its billowing clouds seem to support these long stems, which flower so profusely all summer long, and sway with the lightest breath of wind. African tender fountain grass (*Pennisetum setaceum*) with its fluffy reddish-colored flower spikes is somewhat more robust, but is not frost hardy. 'Sauce Hollandaise' is the name of this variety of golden chamomile (*Anthemis tinctoria*), and looks very similar to true chamomile. The background is composed of groups of fernleaf yarrow (*Achillea filipendulina*) with their corymbs of yellow and creamy-white flowers. Plume poppies (*Macleaya cordata*) on the right complete this summery scene with their striking heart-shaped leaves and sprays of feathery flowers. They can spread rapidly if unchecked, so it is advisable to install some sort of root barrier when planting, similar to that used for bamboo.

Stone by Andrew Loudon, Coniston, GB
Plants Beetham Nurseries, Beetham, GB
Location Tatton Hall Park, Knutsford, GB

Big is beautiful

Anyone can plant a container in the front garden with geraniums, busy lizzies or spheres of box. We see them everywhere, whether in terracotta, frost-resistant terracast or some other material. It is not an unusual way to greet visitors, or even to impress them. But to make a memorable impression, our front gardens need something more original, something a bit different.

The garden

These pots alone make a lasting impression when placed by the entrance to house or garden, and do not require nearly as much attention as one would imagine. Those who say that just one such container would suffice have rather missed the point. The current style is to have very slightly more than the absolute minimum. The containers are dramatic. Made from double-walled zinc with a zinc collar, they stand some 2½ ft (80 cm) tall, which is a perfect height, and should be more commonly available. A tip: roses, which have a deep root system, flourish in deeper than standard containers. Taller containers bring us closer to the plants, so we can look more closely at the leaves and enjoy the scent of the flowers. Maintenance is easier; weeding is more comfortably done at this level, but why three identical pots side by side? They exude an air of abundance. We tend to give and display what we ourselves like. The planting scheme, of course, is a matter of personal choice. Fenna Graf opted for plantain lilies (*Hosta-tardiflora-hybrid 'Halcyon'*) with their steely blue, beautifully textured leaves, which can be looked at closely, and even touched. Some containers of this height and width come with inserts about of the height of the pot, which precludes the

need to use so much compost; these particular containers are full of soil to make them stable. The hostas, as we can see, are very happy in the dappled shade of the honeysuckle. This has been their home for many years.

The loveliest hostas

Hostas are popular precisely because they are uncomplicated foliage perennials. There are thousands of varieties, with new ones being introduced every year. There are many different shapes, sizes and textures of leaf, and also variations in the color and scent of the flowers. Hostas are widely available, but specialist nurseries are recommended. Dr Ullrich Fischer, for example, stocks a wide variety and offers comprehensive professional advice. Contact him at: Waterloostr. 19, 38106 Braunschweig, Tel: +49 531 33 41 10 (www.gartenliteratur.de/pflanzen/hosta). For online sales of hostas (without advice) try Ter Aar near Nieuwveen, Holland (www.hostaparadise.com).

Garden design   Fenna R. Graf, Ascheberg, Ger
Location   Ascheberg, Ger

So little can mean so much: it can be at once inviting, breathtaking, welcoming. Oversized containers are an unexpected touch, especially when planted with these beautiful 'Halcyon' hostas.

Chill-out room

Chilling out is now a widely accepted term for relaxation. The concept of a chill-out room has even made it into the dictionary, although it normally applies to lounges and beachclubs rather than gardens. In fact, a garden is just the place to lounge around doing nothing, as long as the thought of all the gardening chores does not stress you out, or maybe you like to unwind by pulling on a pair of jeans and pottering around doing a bit of pruning, weeding or mowing. Chilling out requires nothing more than comfortable surroundings, with a congenial atmosphere and relaxing background sounds. Water is a good source of the latter, whether trickling or cascading. It makes a pleasing, yet quiet, sound. In areas where traffic noise can be a problem, some gardeners have been known to install features with the sound level of a waterfall to drown out the ambient noise.

The design

This garden, or chill-out room, has famous forebears. Paul Martin was inspired by architect Frank Lloyd Wright's (1867–1953) famous house Fallingwater, built over 70 years ago in Pennsylvania. This private residence was constructed directly over a waterfall. Its organic design makes it fitting that a stream should flow beneath it and emerge as a visible waterfall. Martin modified the idea somewhat in his design by using gabions filled with layers of sandstone slabs to build a wall, leaving a space for a wall of cascading water. The water collects in a splash pool at the bottom of the cascade, and flows under a wooden jetty onto a horizontal glass plate, along which it bubbles for about 3 ft (1 m), before trickling gently into the pool.

The garden

Here is nearly 600 ft square (180 m²) of garden whose only aim is to please. Nearly all the lines are gently curving. The 16 ft (5 m) pool lies very slightly off-center, with sandstone paving slabs following its curved lines. The adjoining path leads away beyond the waterfall. To ensure that the break in the planting is not too pronounced, the designer has installed 10-inch wide x 3-inch high (25 x 8 cm) planks of hardwood, separated by wide gaps, each oriented towards the center of the pool. The planting scheme is bright and varied. Tall bamboo (*Phyllostachys*) facilitates the eye's transition from the high gabion wall to the herbaceous border below, in which we see false goat's beard (*Astilbe*), yellow-margined hostas, and blackroot (*Veronicastrum*), not forgetting the scented annual tobacco plant (*Nicotiana silvestris*) and an olive tree .

Garden design   Paul Martin, Dublin, IRL
Location   Hampton Court, GB

A round peg in a square hole

Everything there is to say about spheres in the garden has probably already been said. The embodiment of perfection, this shape has inspired creative imaginations through the ages. A sphere represents the world as a whole, both nature and civilization, and has echoes of a crystal ball used to foretell the future. Spherical objects are prominent in our lives, so why not introduce them into the garden? They reflect the beauty of our surroundings. The idea is not new. Colored spheres with mirrored surfaces, known as gazing balls, were particularly popular during the Biedermeier period. Their shimmering colored reflections make them an object of fascination, especially in the winter garden, when most flowers are dead and the earth is black.

The garden

This glassy sphere stops the observer in his tracks. The garden boasts some interesting planting and is skillfully designed, but it is the sphere which arrests the eye. This Aqualens radiates an air of freshness and well-being. In an unusual touch, water flows almost imperceptibly over the top of the acrylic sphere, and rather than forming droplets, it covers the sphere like a thin layer of film, then falls gently into the dish below, making no waves. The dish and the platform on which the sphere sits have a polished steel finish which casts magnificent reflections. When the water flows gently, the clouds and the surrounding garden can be seen clearly in them; if the pump is turned up, waves begin to form. Frosty winter weather turns it into a dramatic ice-sculpture. Spare a glance, too, for the garden beyond, with its white-colored plants. A 6½ ft (2 m) obelisk, also designed by Allison Armour, goes almost unnoticed in the right hand corner. All its surfaces are mirrored, elegantly reflecting the imaginative planting scheme, and giving an unexpected depth to the garden.

The details

The spherical Aqualens is made from acrylic glass, and is 24 inches (60 cm) in diameter. It sits on a stainless steel platform, giving the observer the impression that it is hovering above the circular pool, also made of steel. The pool can be sunk into the lawn, or set into a terrace or any other firm base. An electrical connection is required for the pump which circulates the water and makes it run down the sphere (and also for any lighting, if desired). Slow-release chlorine tablets inhibit the build-up of algae.

Garden design	Peter Rogers, GB
Sculptures	Allison Armour, Rusper, GB
Location	Limpsfield, GB

A room with a view

Small outbuildings in the gardens and parks have a long tradition of serving as meeting places, and for sharing special moments with special people. The tea pavilions in the grounds of Schloss Glienicke, the summer palace of Prince Carl of Prussia, would certainly fit this description, with their magnificent views of the Avenue connecting Potsdam and Berlin. It is better known as the "Kleine Neugierde", the "Small Curiosity"; small buildings such as this were erected wherever the view was thought to merit it. Garden owners today are just as inquisitive, but are prevented by building regulations from erecting a garden outbuilding just anywhere.

The garden room

This modern summerhouse has little in common with the classical garden pavilion. The gazebo can be erected even in a small space, and would be suitable for use in any style of garden. The floor measures 11½ x 11½ ft (3.5 x 3.5 m), and the construction is of wood. It is only a transparent shell, ready to be used for any purpose. A narrow staircase links the garden room at ground level with the raised terrace on the second floor. This is a lovely, sunny space with beautiful views. The wooden trellis-work walls can stay see-through as they are, or they could be encircled with climbing, twining plants. Everything can be changed according to individual taste. The frame can be softwood or hardwood, the decor can be minimalist or lavishly opulent, the style rustic or, as in this case, incorporating a touch of the exotic.

Garden design   Andreas Damm, Dirk Schekatz, Aquercus Garten-
        und Landschaftsarchitektur, Heinschenwalde, Ger
Location   Park & Garden Country Fair, Stocksee, Ger;
        currently at the Arboretum Ellerhoop, Ger

The means is the end

The best gardens are full of surprises. The better the planning and construction, the more interesting and unexpected the effect. This first became accepted practice centuries ago, when avenues of trees were planted in such a way that they seemed to stretch into infinity. There are a number of devices one can use to lead the visitor into thinking that the shape or lie of the garden is not as it really is; an upward slope makes the garden appear more spacious than a flat surface or downward incline; creating several garden rooms separated by walls or high hedges also gives the illusion of more space. It is wrong to assume that, to make the most of the available garden space, it all has to be visible at once.

The garden

The illusion within this garden is created by its network of pathways. A central part of the design was its main axis, a path reached through a moon gate at the entrance of the garden area. A second moon gate at the opposite end invites the visitor to take a seat in the area in front of the red sandstone disc. According to traditional Chinese principles, the visitor needs to step through the exact center of a moon gate to symbolize their passage into another world. The paths leading to this point make an irritating number of detours. Paths and plinths of different widths lead up and down steps and, even off to the side. Luckily, the Travertine marble moon gate in its bronze surround is so big as to be unmissable, although the lavish planting along the way sometimes hides it from view. This consists of a splendid selection of perennials and grasses which happen to be in fashion and which reach their peak in May and June. Giant feather grass (*Stipa gigantea*) is soft and gentle, yet towers over the rest of the plants. Its flowers can reach eye-level, and here, they almost reach the moon gate. They underline the lightness and refreshing modern touches of the planting concept.

The plants

Greater masterwort (*Astrantia major* 'Roma') dominates in the foreground. One of the best varieties has old-rose colored blossoms, and often flowers right through to October. The white blooms of Siberian iris (*Iris sibirica* 'White Swirl') can be seen rising above them, accompanied by a number of different white flowers: the poisonous ameus (*Ammi majus*), orlayas, and marguerites (*Leucanthemum vulgare*). In the background, and on the opposite side is a display of Bowman's root (*Gillenia trifoliata*), which flowers all summer long, then takes on a different guise in fall, when its foliage turns red. The stems are also very attractive.

Garden design   Jinny Blom, London, GB
Location   London, GB

The path leading to the seat at the end
of the garden is not clearly defined,
but the grasses and flowers on the way
make it idyllic.

Setting the scene

The success of a garden's design should be measured not just in broad daylight, or in spring, when crocus and tulips are in full bloom, or even in summer, when the borders are chock-full of color: a good design also proves its worth at night, when the paths are lit and the space becomes like a stage set ready for the show to begin. It is no easy task, but the results are worth the effort.

The garden

This house and its living space can be entirely open to the outdoors. The clients wanted to experience their garden to the full. The glass doors can be fully closed or fully open, depending on the weather and the time of year. It is almost like being outside all year round. The still water of the pool casts wonderful reflections. The views and the reflections of the clouds are magnificent from every part of the glass house, while the view from the garden into the house is equally attractive. In an effort not to waste the hours during which the seating areas, pools and plants are bathed in darkness, an imaginative pattern of lighting has been installed, reminiscent of lighting up a stage. The light cast by the house at night plays an integral part. The scheme is underpinned by beams of light emanating from underneath the glass extension and lighting up the pool. A number of features have been accorded their own individual spotlights, the sweetgum tree in the foreground (*Liquidambar styraciflua*) to name but one. Even in the daytime, its bright red foliage seems to radiate light. Why on earth would anyone want to forego the delight of

seeing this marvelous redness enhanced by energy saving lighting, or of seeing the shrubs and perennials from a new perspective against an illuminated wall? There could only be one reason, a financial one.

More light, but keep it gentle!

Well-positioned lights can make the night garden look larger. In-ground uplighters can be used to highlight tree trunks and canopies, pergolas, seating areas, walls and façades. They can be controlled remotely from the house. Downlighters are perfect for paths, while a directional spotlight provides ambient light. These are all available as low-voltage models. There is a very wide range of 12 volt halogen lights available, suitable for a narrow spotlight beam of 8° to a broad floodlight of 60°. The low-voltage cable is connected to a 230 volt mains cable via a transformer. The scheme shown here is effective not because of the amount of light it radiates, but because of the skillful interplay of light and shadow, which gives the garden a wonderfully substantial feel.

Ingenieurbüro für Lichttechnik Rüdiger Noelle, 24576 Hitzhusen, Germany
www.nightscaping.de.

Garden design Henk Weijers (†), Haarlem, NL
Location Ramelsloh, Ger

A garden for the senses

Copper is a sought-after metal, commanding top prices on the international market. Even in the garden, copper has broken free from its traditional supporting role in water features and weather vanes, and is displaying a new, bright and polished side to its character. Not only is it practical, it looks attractive too. Why not use copper pipes purely for their decorative effect, and show off the shiny brilliance of this versatile metal?

The garden

When this sunken garden is used in the way the designer envisaged, it represents the four elements: fire, water, air and earth. The discrete rounded space in the background houses a barbecue area, where 6–8 people can sit comfortably around the fire, while the low Yorkshire sandstone wall can easily accommodate more guests. Water, too, plays and important, even a decisive, part in the design, and is present on both levels. The upper plateau can be seen in the foreground in this photograph. The pool up here is enclosed almost entirely by walls capped with sawn plinths of sandstone. The wall is broken off for a matter of 7–8 ft (2–3 m) however, and replaced by a copper plinth. Water flows down this plinth to the level of the sunken patio, but there is more: in the center of the lower pool, a single olive tree stands alone on an island. The designer wanted to add a touch of the Mediterranean. Air is the third element, of which there is no shortage, while earth can be found all around in the borders where shrubs and flowering perennials thrive. The seven copper pipes (nine altogether) punctuate the reflections from the still water, provide a strong architectural component, and contrast sharply with the white walls.

Copper

Copper was the earliest metal known to man. There is evidence to show that it was being used 8,000 years ago. It occurs naturally in varying concentrations. The ancient Romans called it the "metal of Cyprus", after the area where it was intensively mined at that time. Copper has a wide variety of applications, as pipes for drinking water, for example, or for gas or oil, or even for domestic drainpipes. Untreated copper oxidizes on contact with moist air, although oxidation can be prevented by applying a clear varnish. The oxidation process causes the metal to change color from a reddish brown to slate-gray. Combined with other metals, copper can make some interesting alloys, bronze probably being the best known. Bronze is an alloy of copper and tin, so widely used that it has an era of history named after it (around 1600–1200 BC). The combination of copper and zinc makes up the hard, shiny alloy we know today as brass.

Garden design   D. C. Duiker-Parker, GB

Location   Tatton Park, Knutsford, GB

Garden art

Art in the garden is an important concept. Artists see open spaces, plants and materials from a different perspective – perhaps slightly more distanced from them than garden professionals, or even amateur gardeners, for whom the garden is part of everyday life.

The concept of "Vocabulum Hortus – Villandry"

Inspired by the topiary garden in the Garden of Love at Château de Villandry, this design is created out of local sandstone from Anröchte, set into the center of a sand garden, and framed with a border of blue and green plants. Visitors to France are probably familiar with the 16th century Château, which is famous above all for its innovative vegetable garden. Cabbages, lettuces and onions are grouped together according to color, and planted in squares like flowers in a border. The love garden is on the level above the kitchen garden. Symbols for different kinds of love have been skillfully shaped from box bushes, and this was the inspiration for the garden in the photograph. A motif was sawn from a 10 ft (3 m) square of sandstone, then the square garden was enlarged, again taking its inspiration from the Château, using a grid pattern. A strip of sand was added, then a 24-inch wide (60 cm) band of sandstone, and then more sand. Finally, a flowerbed planted with blue-gray grasses and blue flowering perennials takes the garden out to its boundaries. The repetition of the increasing geometric pattern can be explained thus: the observer moves back and forth between the idea of the prosaic everyday use of a sand box and the perception of the small plastic shapes placed at regular intervals, colored blue to match the plants. He is encouraged to consider the sensual nature of the garden. At the moment, the blue fescue (*Festuca cinerea* 'Azurit' and 'Glauca') are at their peak, but will soon be succeeded by garden speedwell (*Veronica longifolia* 'Blue Giantess'), fairy's thimbles (*Campanula cochleariifolia*) and *Salvia* 'Blauhügel' and 'Mainacht'. Baroque and minimalism go hand in hand here, as contemporary shapes sit happily side by side with historical motifs. The garden received a special award.

Green sandstone from Anröchte

This sandstone was formed some 120 million years ago from sand deposited in the primordial ocean at Anröchte, as evidenced by the fossilized corals, seashells and snail shells frequently found therein. The mineral glaukonit is responsible for the sandstone's unique color. When the stone is quarried, the green strata are separated from the white. For retail purposes, it is sometimes classified as a dolomite, which is not, however, an accurate description. In the "Hortus Villandry" the stone has first been sculpted, then sandblasted using quartz sand, leaving a textured, grainy finish. Natursteinvertrieb Schulte, Anröchte, www.schulte-naturstein.de.

Garden design   Insa Winkler, Gerd Kunis, Kunst & Landschaft, Hude, Ger
Location   Park & Garden Country Fair, Stocksee, Ger

The garden lounge

The pergola is dead, long live the lounge! Stylistically speaking, it is fairly clear in which direction the romantic notion of foliage-clad summerhouses is being pushed by the crisp lines of the garden room. The architectural style of new-build housing has changed, and so must the style of any garden buildings that go with it. There are plenty of plants all around, so why should we need roses to push their way right up to our table, or spiders to torment our (mainly female) guests? It is bad enough having to cope with the midges when we sit out on the patio in the evenings.

The concept

From one point of view, this contemporary garden room is a real eyecatcher. It has clean lines, and seems to float above the plants. It is practical too; ideal on a hot summer's day. Rain will not stop play, and neither will the evening dew as it descends onto the garden, the transparent plexiglass roof will see to that. The steel structure is designed to look unconstricted and unconstricting. This outdoor room measures some 20 x 10 x 8 ft (6 x 3 x 2.4 m). One side is enclosed by a wall, giving it a feeling of security. Three ceramic sculptures by Mari-Ruth Oda, and the modern seating modules (Aqua Collection by Paula Lenti) highlight the way we respond to modern life today in natural surroundings. The unusual wood sculpture winds through the whole garden, linking its different areas. The theme of the garden is Cancer Research's "Together we will beat cancer" campaign from the UK. Andy Sturgeon designed the flowing sculpture which was then made by Sixixis. Three strands of oak, each measuring 4 x 1 inches (10 x 3 cm) and each 100 ft (30 m) long were bent into these infinite shapes using a steam bending method. In just a short time, the perennial plants and the wooden sculpture will meld into a single entity, and will add a little privacy to this outdoor lounge.

The plants

The woody shrub dominating in the background here is the giant dogwood (*Cornus controversa*), quite possibly one of the loveliest small trees around. Its tiered branches are a striking feature, as are its many clusters of white flowers in June. More perennials swirl around the base of the wooden sculpture. Heavenly bamboo (*Nandina domestica*) sits well next to the beautiful blue of the woodland sage (*Salvia nemorosa* 'May Night') and the dramatic spiny bear's breech (*Acanthus spinosus*), while behind it, the background consists of globe artichoke (*Cynara cardunculus*) with its silvery-gray leaves, and clumps of pheasant's tail grass (*Stipa arundinacea*). The small plants in front of the pavilion consists of the dark purple flowers of wild sage (*Salvia nemorosa* 'Caradonna') the rarely-seen columbine (*Aquilegia vulgaris* 'Black Barlow') with its unusually dark brownish-purple flowers, and more feather grass (*Stipa*).

Garden design   Andy Sturgeon, Brighton, GB
Location   London, GB

Eyecatchers

Everyone likes surprises, but most gardens contain very few of them. Tranquility is one thing, but nothing except rolling lawns and rose bushes? The more adventurous amongst us could find that a little boring. The addition of a focal point, some sort of eye catcher, would give it a spark of life. A garden should, after all, be stimulating.

The garden

How about some empty plant pots as a decorative feature? Not such a strange idea if they look like this. These must be some of the most unusual and dramatic available, both in terms of shape and materials. They look as light as an ice-cream cone, or a ballerina en pointe, yet are firmly anchored to the ground, and seem to hover above this small garden space. They are made of copper, and already show signs of the attractive patina which forms on the surface after exposure to air. They tone beautifully with the red-leaved plants in the background, from the left purple-leaved weeping beech (*Fagus sylvatica* 'Purpurea Pendula'), Japanese maple (*Acer palmatum* 'Fireglow') and Thunberg's barberry (*Berberis thunbergii* 'Red Chief'). The plantain lilies (*Hosta* 'Big Daddy') with their round or heart-shaped leaves were an inspired choice for the copper containers. The color contrast is striking. The surface of the pots is mulched with gravel to match the paths, a professional finishing touch.

Garden design	James Dyson, Jim Honey (Gardenvista), Hove, GB
Location	London, GB

Health and well-being

The sauna has competition! Anyone interested in improving their day-to-day health is on the lookout for additional ways to complement their daily fitness routine, and visits to the sauna are one such way, but try to imagine a having a massage in your own private whirlpool in the garden. This would be relaxation in its purest form, yet a trend which is quite easily achievable. The usual reason for buying a whirlpool is to relive happy memories of relaxing in a spa on vacation. For a real spa experience, try a break in the Belgian town of Spa. This was the original spa break, famed as early as the 16th century for the healing properties of its water. The British were among the first to appreciate its special powers.

into the garden. The unusual angle gives the garden an even more interesting perspective, and while you are relaxing in the warm pool being massaged by jets of water, you can rest assured that you are actively enhancing your own well-being, and even your health. After a session in the whirlpool, why not take a warm shower, in the knowledge that the water has been heated by solar panels.

The garden

This is a different take on the patio as an activity center. A whirlpool is an unusual garden feature, but there is every reason to suppose that its popularity is on the increase. It can be incorporated into even the smallest space, as this design shows. The area is reminiscent of a courtyard garden, with every square inch put to good use. Only the very edges of the garden, and a few islands (in front of the conservatory, for instance) are planted with sun-loving perennials and Mediterranean favorites such as rosemary and sage. Blocks of natural stone within the beds provide seating. The hard landscaping consists of granite-finished pavers of varying lengths, which give the illusion of space in this fairly small area, although enough room has been found for a table and chairs. In the middle of the paved area the surface changes to wood, with a whirlpool sunk into its center. The bathing and spa area is, in fact, elliptical in shape, inlaid diagonally

A whirlpool in the garden

However appealing the idea of a private spa area in your back garden, complete with a hot tub of bubbling water, it is important to draw up the design carefully. A comparison with the porch swing springs to mind: it is only attractive when in use, an eyesore when covered. As it is imperative that the whirlpool remains covered when not in use, it is important to position it well away from the living room window. The pool remains filled throughout the winter, with water at a temperature of about 97 °F (36 °C), as a hot tub is particularly enjoyable on a cold winter's day. To keep the water clean, the pH values need to be monitored daily. A self-administering dosing device is highly recommended. More info: Pichler Kunststofftechnik, Eggenfelden, www.pichler.de.

Garden design   John Everiss und Peter Gregory, GB

Location   Cirencester, GB

The green belt

Bamboo is gradually taking over the western world, both as a living plant and in the form of furniture, flooring, and in the near future, as a versatile building material. The range of bamboo types currently available is huge. Even their unusual flowering patterns, leading directly to their death, have not dampened our enthusiasm. It may be that the mysterious nature of bamboo blossoms and their link to the demise of the plant is the very feature that fuels our interest.

The garden

This small segment of garden from the grounds of Stockseehof could be an off-site advertisement for Hamburg's Botanical Garden, as the latter has a penchant for bamboo, and plans are in the pipeline for a Chinese Scholar's garden. The central feature in this 23 ft (7 m) garden is an extraordinary natural stone fountain, made of Anröchte sandstone (Qi-Objects, Braunschweig, www.qi-objects.de). It measures about 6½ x 3 x 2½ ft (2 x 0.95 x 0.8 m) and weighs some 2.8 tonnes. Water bubbles up from a recess on the left hand side, over an angled sill and then down the front face of the stone, trickling away between the small, irregular stone slabs at the base. The water is circulated artificially using an electric pump. A large circular hole has been bored right through the stone, on the right hand side, through which Japanese maple is growing (*Acer palmatum*). 20 ft (6 m) bamboo plants (*Phyllostachys aureosulcata* 'Spectabilis') with their golden yellow canes featuring green stripes are planted as boundary markers. These would be dramatic even if they grew in containers. Dwarf bamboo (*Sasa pumila*), which requires constant support, accompanies the visitor on the approach to the fountain. Granite chippings cover the ground, giving the bamboo a decorative base from which to grow. 28 inch (70 cm) PECD rhizome barriers are hidden under the ground to prevent bamboo canes appearing in unwanted places. The garden was constructed by Garten + Raum, 23845 Seth (www.gartenundraum.de). NB: This garden is available for viewing during the summer, along with "Welcome to Scandinavia!" and "Garden art" (www.stockseehof.de).

Bamboo

- A wide range of bamboo types is available at Bambus Centrum Deutschland, Saarstrasse 3–5, 76532 Baden-Baden, www.bambus.de/eberts; Bambus-Informationszentrum, Ramhorster Strasse 2, 31275 Lehrte-Steinwedel, www.bambus-info.de, who also supplied this garden.

- Bamboo for viewing: Hamburg Botanical Garden, Ohnhorststrasse 18, 22609 Hamburg.
- Bamboo News: "Bambus Journal" for members of the European Bamboo Society (German Section), published quarterly (www.bambus-deutschland.de). Website provides links to international bamboo organizations.

Garden design	Ulrich Timm, Hamburg, Ger
Implementation	Qi-Objects, Braunschweig, Ger; Simon Herda, Garten + Raum, Seth, Ger
Location	Park & Garden Country Fair, Stocksee, Ger

More than just a game

The game of chess has a long history. Something similar was played in India, but the game we know today evolved from a Persian invention in the middle ages, and made its way to Europe via the Arab states. The distinctive board developed along with the game. It is a work of art in itself. It consists of 64 squares of alternating colors; black and white are usual, but any dark and light shades would be appropriate. Garden chess has its loyal band of followers, but is not a game to be played at the table; the pieces on the walk-on chessboard (usually made from concrete or natural stone pavers, or even a synthetic material, skillfully joined together) are about half the size of the players.

The concept

The gardens of Château du Rivau on the Loire have always been inspiring, even as early as the 16th century. The "potager", or kitchen garden, is particularly impressive. The current owner is Patricia Laigneau, artist and landscape designer. She felt it was important to do more than just maintain the status quo; she wanted to add her own modern touches. One of these was to plant a flower garden in the pattern of a checkerboard. The garden is laid out on the site of some outbuildings which formerly enclosed the castle's front courtyard. This is a modern interpretation rather than a faithful replica of a checkerboard, and since the game has its roots in the middle ages, it is quite appropriate in this setting. Instead of 64 squares, this board has only 56, but they are larger than normal, at nearly 5 ft (1.5 m) square, enclosed in squared timber frames, which makes them big enough to accommodate David Austin's English shrub

roses. 20 squares are planted with three roses each; the varieties chosen have the flower shape of a traditional rose, but they have an intense fragrance, and bloom all summer long (traditional rose varieties only bloom once a year). The rose squares are topped with a 4 inch (10 cm) layer of light mulch, which is especially visible in winter and spring, after pruning work has been carried out and the perennials are cut back. The mulch helps the soil to retain moisture, inhibits weed growth and serves to distinguish these squares from the ones planted with grass, lavender or herbaceous perennials. This is one of the attractions of a checkerboard pattern: it gives a good basic structure, which can be changed according to taste. Maintenance, however, is high. The edges of the squares have to remain clearly visible.

Tip

If you want to continue the checkerboard theme in your own garden, you could try planting some of the squares with flowering bulbs, particularly checkered lily (*Fritillaria meleagris*), a relative of the crown imperial. It has a very pretty, evenly-checkered bell-shaped flower atop a stem of up to 10 inches (25 cm) tall, and is currently en vogue. It will thrive in any partially-shaded spot which does not dry out in summer.

Garden design   Patricia Laigneau, Lémeré, F
Location   Château du Rivau, Lémeré, F

Checkerboard planting makes an enchanting
pattern. It can be large or small, indoors or out.
The pattern is clear and straightforward, and
can have a calming effect.

A place to meditate

Once in a while, garden designs should push back the barriers of tradition. They should use unusual materials to create an unexpected atmosphere which encourages contemplation. If visitors have the time and inclination to join in, they could even meditate in a show garden. And what material could have this effect? Glass, crushed of course.

The garden

The two American designers call their design "Desert Sea", but it goes far beyond this concept. Vietnamese-born Andy Cao has brought his childhood experiences of home into his work. The designers shipped several miles of rope along with many tons of glass in the form of recycled glass, pebbles and marbles to the Loire Valley in France the site of the exhibition. The rope was used to build a 6½ ft (2 m) high wall as a backdrop, enclosing the space in which they constructed their miniature landscape, an island studded with spiky cacti in a sea of bright blue "water". Glass orbs stand in a pool of real water, balanced on rope-wrapped pedestals, also studded with cacti and echeveria. They are reminiscent of Vietnamese water puppets. The design was inspired by the dry garden at the temple in Ryoan-jin in Kyoto. The designers were the first to appreciate the potential of colored glass as an artist's medium for contemplative spaces.

Garden design   Andy Cao, Stephen Jerrom, Los Angeles, USA

Location   Festival des Jardins de Chaumont-sur-Loire, F

The revival of the knot garden

Knot gardens have an intrinsic mysterious quality, as if they are concealing something precious. Their patterns, their fragrance, their carefully chosen planting scheme and the way their hedges are woven and interwoven all contribute to their unique atmosphere. It can be startling to see a motif, so familiar to us from embroideries and tapestries of bygone days, reproduced in three dimensions using low hedging. One of the loveliest knot gardens of recent times was designed and planted by the late Rosemary Verey in her famous garden in Gloucestershire, England. This beautiful piece of landscaping belongs to Barnsley House, now a luxury hotel.

The garden

The owner of Château du Rivau on the Loire first had the idea for a knot garden while examining some of the documents relating to the origins of the Château at the time of the Renaissance, between 1400 and 1600. Although knot gardens were established at around this time, this one has a very modern feel to it, giving the Château grounds that extra something. It is a revival, but in contemporary style. Patricia Laigneau recognized that a knot garden incorporates a great many modern traits. The plants are geometric, the choice of plants reined in to minimalist proportions and the planting scheme is highly creative, as befits this artist turned garden designer. Only lavender (*Lavandula angustifolia* ssp. *angustifolia*) and silver-leaved cotton lavender (*Santolina chamaecyparissus*) are planted here, weaving a timeless carpet in the gravel bed. The interplay of different shades of green is highly effective, whether the lavender is in bud, as in the photo, or in full bloom. Rosemary Verney, on the other hand, used four different species: green and yellow box (*Buxus sempervirens* 'Suffruticosa' and 'Aureovariegata'), cotton lavender (*Santolina chamaecyparissus*) and germander (*Teucrium × lucydris*).

The history of knot gardens

Knot gardens, with their low hedges laid out in geometric and symmetrical patterns, became fashionable in the 16th century, and were often featured in the grounds of country houses and palaces. The English called them knot gardens, while the French preferred the term "parterres de broderie". They mostly incorporated patterns found in embroideries and tapestries, but family crests were also frequently found planted in outline in the garden. Knot gardens are popular today mainly for their visual appeal, but historically their purpose was more therapeutic. Box was combined with lavender; a little thyme and summer savory was added, and the whole was enclosed by a low yew hedge. The correct arrangement of these elements, it was said, could bring man into harmony with the cosmos.

Garden design   Patricia Laigneau, Lémeré, F
Location   Château du Rivau, Lémeré, F

Transparency

It is unusual to see a dividing wall in the center of the garden, but the barrier has been placed here for logical reasons, and should not be seen as an insurmountable hurdle. The designer's intention was quite the reverse in fact. She chose to use plexiglass, sandblasted to give a velvety-smooth, matt, yet translucent surface, and the gaps between them are there to be used.

The garden

This is a theme full of tension and excitement; two gardens in one. Two German gardens, in fact, one leaning more towards the east, the other in a western style. It may seem clichéd, but nevertheless has its roots in reality. A fixed screen prevents the two sides from being united. A number of 6½ x 6½ ft (2 x 2 m) aluminum frames are set at 2½ ft intervals. Each holds a translucent sheet of plexiglass, ¼ inch (5 mm) thick, so we can only just make out what is happening on the other side. Clearly discernible silhouettes heighten the tension, as when twigs and branches cast their shadows on to glass walls. Prepare for the unexpected as you step through the opening; the layout of the gardens is similar, but the plant content is very different indeed. The western side on the right (in the foreground of the photograph) contains perennials and grasses with attractive flowers, grown solely for visual appeal. Starting from the left, we see esparto grass (*Stipa tenacissima*), avens (*Geum coccineum* 'Borisii') and bearded iris (*Iris barbata*), with a staghorn sumach (*Rhus typhina*) as a specimen tree. The East garden on the far side of the dividing line contains mainly edible plants, such as kitchen herbs, lettuce and asparagus. The specimen tree here is a quince.

The eastern plants

Laid out in rows: feather reed grass (*Calamagrostis × acutiflora* 'Karl Foerster'), tall prairie tickseed (*Coreopsis tripteris*), kalimeris (*Kalimeris incisa*), asparagus, golden marjoram, (*Origanum vulgare* 'Aureum'), chives, parsley, silver tansy (*Tanacetum niveum* 'Jackpot'), garden rue (*Ruta graveolens* 'Jackpot Blue'), hyssop, and finally some flowering marigolds.

The western plants

In parallel, also laid out in rows: orange sneezeweed (*Helenium* 'Baudirektor Lange'), panic grass (*Panicum* 'Hänse Herms'), coneflower (*Rudbeckia deamii*), *Pennisetum compressum*, gaura (*Gaura lindheimeri*), Shasta daisy (*Leucanthemum maximum* 'Christine Hagemann') Chinese fountain grass, golden chamomile (*Anthemis tinctoria*), red scabious (*Knautia macedonica*), esparto grass (*Stipa tenacissima*), cranesbill (*Geranium* 'Jolly Bee'), baby's breath (*Gypsophila* 'Rosenschleier'), bearded iris, and avens (*Geum coccineum* 'Borisii').

Garden design   Petra Pelz, Magdeburg, Ger

Location   Park & Garden Country Fair, Stocksee, Ger

Index

A

Acacia 162, 164

Acanthus spinosus 186

Acer 164

Acer campestre 62, 146

Acer palmatum 62, 148, 188, 192

Acer palmatum 'Dissectum atropurpureum' 148

Acer palmatum 'Fireglow' 188

Acer platanoides 'Globosum' 160

Achillea 'Terracotta' 94

Achillea filipendulina 168

Aconitum carmichaelii × 'Arendsii' 48

African tender fountain grass 100, 168

African lily 24, 158

Agapanthus 24, 158

Agapanthus africanus 'Headbourne' 24

Agave Americana 'Glauca' 86

Ailanthus altissima 54

Alchemilla 126

Alchemilla mollis 38, 48

Algae 36, 106

Allium 5, 28, 108, 138, 140, 154, 158, 160

Allium 'Globemaster' 28, 140

Allium 'Mont Blanc' 154, 158

Allium 'Mount Everest' 28, 138

Allium 'Purple Sensation' 28, 140, 160

Allium giganticum 140

Allium karataviense 140

Allium stipitatum 140

Allium christophii 140

Allium sphaerocephalon 28

Alisma plantago-aquatica 30

Alumroot 12, 38, 148

Amelanchier lamarckii 126, 134, 146

American arbor vitae 16

Ameus 178

Ammi majus 178

Anchusa italica 'Loddon Royalist' 90

Angelica 112

Anthemis tinctoria 168, 200

Antirrhinum 134

Apple 22, 96

Aquilegia vulgaris 'Black Barlow' 186

Aquilegia-vulgaris-hybrid 'Black Barlow' 148

Aralia elata 160

Arrowhead 36

Artemisia 94, 104, 152

Asarum europaeum 130

Asparagus 200

Aster × *frikartii* 'Wunder von Stäfa' 142

Astilbe 172

Astilbe arendsii 'White Gloria' 164

Astrantia 8

Astrantia major 'Claret' 146

Astrantia major 'Roma' 178

Australian tree fern 148

Austrian black pine 146

Avena 136

Avens 152, 168, 200

Azalea 58

B

Baby's breath 142, 200

Baby's tears 108

Bamboo 50, 56, 86, 100, 148, 168, 172, 192

Bearberry cotoneaster 102

Beard tongue 104

Bearded iris 64, 138, 200

Beech 16, 24, 32

Bellflower 164

Berberis thunbergii 'Bagatelle' 160

Berberis thunbergii 'Red Chief' 188

Bergenia 104

Betula utilis 48, 64, 130

Betula utilis 'Doorenbos' 64

Betula utilis var. *jaquemontii* 'Doorenbos' 130

Birch 130, 138

Bishop's hat 108

Bistorta officinalis 'Superba' 90

Black bamboo 148

Black dragon 148

Black locust 160

Blackroot 172

Bleeding heart 142

Blue fescue 184

Blue moor grass 90

Blue Scots pine 146

Bluebeard 134

Blue-ringed aloe 86

Bonsai 70, 100, 148

Bowman's root 178

Box 5, 8, 10, 16, 18, 22, 24, 28, 30, 32, 44, 46, 50, 54, 56, 58, 62, 66, 70, 98, 102, 118, 120, 122, 126, 132, 138, 150, 154, 158, 170, 184, 198

Buddleja-davidii-hybrids 134

Bugloss 112

Bulrush 36, 132

Burning bush 146

Bush mallow 134

Busy lizzie 46, 170

Butterfly bush 134

Buxus 146

Buxus 'Tide Hill' 66

Buxus sempervirens 8, 70, 102, 146, 154, 198

Buxus sempervirens 'Blauer Heinz' 8

Buxus sempervirens 'Rotundifolia' 8, 70

Buxus sempervirens 'Suffruticosa' 102, 198

Buxus sempervirens var. *arborescens* 8, 146

C

Calamagrostis × *acutiflora* 'Karl Foerster' 44, 90, 142, 200

Camellia 58

Campanula cochleariifolia 184

Canadian hemlock 146

Carex 18, 86, 112, 114, 160

Carex elata 86, 112

Carex elata 'Aurea' 112

Carex morrowii 'Variegata' 18, 114

Carpinus betulus 38, 60, 62, 78, 90, 120, 146, 160

Carpinus betulus 'Fastigiata' 38, 60, 120, 160

Carpinus betulus 'Fransfontaine' 78

Caryopteris × *clandonensis* 134

Catalpa bignonioides 'Nana' 54

Catmint 12, 88, 134, 138, 142

Cattail 84

Chaenomeles-hybrids 134

Chamaecyparis lawsoniana 'Alumii' 24

Checkered lily 194

Index

Cherry 22

Chestnut 164

Chinese fountain grass 142, 200

Chinese silver grass 64, 66, 124, 142

Chives 28, 200

Chrysanthemum maximum 'Gruppenstolz' 44

Chrysanthemum-maximum-hybrid
       'Gruppenstolz' 44, 134

Chusan palm 86

Clematis 'Black Prince' 148

Club palm 110

Coleus 112

Columbine 148, 186

Common columbine 148

Coneflower 12, 142, 200

Cordyline 110

Coreopsis 128, 200

Coreopsis tripteris 200

Cornel 146

Cornelian cherry 160

Cornus alba 'Argenteomarginata' 138

Cornus controversa 186

Cornus kousa 112

Cornus mas 146, 160

Cosmos 44

Cosmos bipinnatus 44

Cotoneaster dammeri 'Skogholm' 102

Cotoneaster × suecicus 'Skogholm' 102

Cotton lavender 104, 160, 198

Crabapple 22, 62, 130, 146, 160

Cranesbill 108, 116, 126

Crataegus laevigata 'Paul Scarlet' 160

Crataegus 'Carrierei' 74

Creeping juniper 144

Crimson midland hawthorn 160

Crocus 22, 28, 180

Culver's root 142

Cynara cardunculus 186

Cyperus 66

Cyperus alternifolius 30

D

Daffodil 28, 140

Dahlia 'Bishop of Llandaff' 26

Day-lily 112, 152

Deschampsia 128

Deschampsia 'Goldschleier' 26

Deschampsia cespitosa 90, 136

Deschampsia cespitosa 'Goldschleier' 136

Dicentra 142

Dicksonia antarctica 148, 164

Digitalis 88, 130, 152, 160

Digitalis purpurea 'Albiflora' 88

Digitalis purpurea 'Saltwood Summer' 130

Dipsacus fullonum 134

Ditchmoss 36

Dogwood 138

Doronicum × excelsum 'Harpur Crewe' 12

Dryopteris erythrosora 148

Dwarf bamboo 192

Dwarf sweet box 60

E

Echinacea purpurea 'Alba' 142

Elderberry 164

Elodea 36

English shrub roses 194

English yew 120

Epimedium 108

Equisetum hyemale 86

Eremurus 152

Erigeron karvinskianus 154

Esparto grass 200

Euonymus alatus 146

Euphorbia amygdaloides var. *robbiae* 138

European beech 156

European hornbeam 38, 60, 62, 160

European wild ginger 130

F

Fagus sylvatica 16, 156, 188

Fagus sylvatica 'Purpurea Pendula' 188

Fairy's thimble 184

False cypress 24

False goat's beard 172

Fargesia 56, 100, 128

Fargesia murieliae 'Smaragd' 56

Fargesia murieliae 128

Feather grass 26, 108, 168, 186

Feather reed grass 90, 142, 200

Fennel 38

Fern 64, 138, 164

Fernleaf yarrow 168

Fescue 'Blauschwingel' 24

Festuca cinerea 24

Festuca cinerea 'Azurit' 184

Festuca cinerea 'Glauca' 184

Field maple 62, 146

Fish-pole bamboo 46

Flag iris 72, 84

Flowering cherry 146

Flowering quince 134

Foeniculum vulgare 'Rubrum' 38

Forsythia 126

Foxglove 88, 130, 152, 160

Foxglove beard-tongue 146

Foxtail lily 152

Fragrant viburnum 134

Fritillaria meleagris 194

G

Garden peony 134

Garden rue 200

Garden speedwell 184

Garlic 28

Gaura 200

Gaura lindheimeri 200

Geranium 108, 116, 126, 148, 170, 200

Geranium 'Jolly Bee' 116, 200

Geranium pretense 'New Dimension' 148

German iris 148

Germander 198

Geum 152

Geum coccineum 168, 200

Geum coccineum 'Borisii' 200

Giant dogwood 186

Giant feather grass 90, 136, 154, 178

Gillenia trifoliata 178

Ginkgo tree 144

Globe artichoke 186

Globe head Norway maple 160

Golden chamomile 168, 200

Index

Golden groundsel 72

Golden marjoram 200

Golden rain 52

Grape hyacinth 116

Greater masterwort 146, 178

Gypsophila 142, 200

Gypsophila 'Rosenschleier' 200

H

Hair cap moss 130

Hair grass 128

Hawthorn 74

Heath pearlwort 106

Heavenly bamboo 186

Hedgehog rose 104

Helenium 'Baudirektor Lange' 200

Helenium 'Moerheim Beauty' 26

Helichrysum 104

Helictotrichon sempervirens 136

Hemerocallis 126, 152

Heuchera cylindrica 12

Heuchera micrantha 'Palace Purple' 38, 148

Himalayan birch 48, 64

Hippophae rhamnoides 104

Holly 100

Holly oak 104

Hollyhock 148

Honeysuckle 128

Hornbeam 78, 90, 120, 132, 146,

Hosta 28, 108, 114, 126, 136, 148, 170, 172

Hosta 'Big Daddy' 188

Hosta sieboldiana 'Frances Williams' 148

Hosta sieboldii 'Alba' 136

Hosta tardiana 'Halcyon' 114

Houseleek 28

Hydrangea 134

Hydrangea paniculata 134

Hydrangea petiolaris 134

Hyssop 200

I

Ilex crenata 100

Impatiens 46

Imperata cylindrical 'Rubra' 136

Indian bean tree 54

Iris barbata 200

Iris ensata 6

Iris pseudacorus 84

Iris pseudacorus 'Ivory' 72

Iris sibirica 'White Swirl' 130, 178

Iris-barbata-elatior-hybrid 'Night Ruler' 148

Iris-barbata-eliator-hybrid 64

Italian bugloss 90

Ivy 58

J

Japanese angelica tree 160

Japanese barberry 160

Japanese blood grass 136

Japanese dogwood 112

Japanese flowering cherry 96

Japanese iris 6

Japanese maple 62, 148, 188, 192

Japanese sedge 18, 114

Japanese shield fern 148

Japanese spurge 50

Juneberry 126, 134, 146

Juniper 144

Jupiter's beard 8

K

Kalimeris 200

Kalimeris incisa 200

Knautia macedonica 90, 200

L

Laburnum 52

Lady's mantle 38, 48, 126

Larch 144

Latin American fleabane 154

Laurel 58

Lavandula angustifolia ssp. *angustifolia* 198

Lavatera thuringiaca 134

Lavatera-olbia-hybrid 'Barnsley' 134

Lavender 104, 126, 194, 198

Lawson's cypress 24

Leatherleaf viburnum 146

Leathery wood-spurge 138

Lettuce 200

Leucanthemum maximum 'Christine Hagemann' 200

Leucanthemum vulgare 178

Lichen 156

Ligularia dentata 'Desdemona' 72

Lilac 134, 164

Lily 140

Linden 82

Liquidambar styraciflua 180

Lombardy poplar 88

Lonicera × *heckrottii* 128

Lupin 134

Lupinus-polyphyllus-hybrid 'Edelknabe' 134

Luzula nivea 88

M

Macleaya cordata 168

Malus 160

Malus 'Evereste' 146, 160

Malus 'Red Sentinel' 62

Maple 18

Marguerite 178

Marigold 134, 200

Meadow cranesbill 148

Medlar 38

Mescal 110

Mespilus cydonia 38

Mexican aster 44

Michaelmas daisies 142

Mirabelle 22

Miscanthus 16, 66, 124, 128, 140, 142

Miscanthus sinensis 'Gracillimus' 66, 124

Miscanthus sinensis 'Malepartus' 142

Mock orange 126, 128, 134

Monkshood 48

Moss 46, 80, 106, 156

Mother-in-law's-tongue 146

Mountain pine 100

Muscari 116

N

Nandina domestica 186

Nasturtium 134

Index

Nepeta × faassenii 'Six Hills Giant' 134, 142
Nepeta × faassenii 'Walker's Low' 12, 88, 134, 138
New Zealand sedge 160
Nicotiana silvestris 172

O
Oatgrass 136
Olea europea 94
Olive tree 94, 100, 172, 182
Orange sneezeweed 200
Oriental poppy 94
Origanum vulgare 'Aureum' 200
Orlaya 178
Ornamental onion 28, 108, 154, 160
Osier 162

P
Pachysandra terminalis 50
Paeonia officinalis 'Rosea Plena' 134
Palm lily 112
Panic grass 200
Panicum 'Hänse Herms' 200
Panicum virgatum 'Cloud Nine' 142
Papaver orientale 94, 142
Papaver orientale 'Orangeade Maison' 94
Papyrus sedge 68
Parsley 200
Pear 22
Pearlwort 106
Pennisetum 100, 128, 142, 168, 200
Pennisetum alopecuroides 128, 142
Pennisetum alopecuroides 'Hameln' 128

Pennisetum compressum 128, 200
Pennisetum setaceum 100, 168
Pennisetum villosum 128
Penstemon 104, 134, 146
Penstemon digitalis 'Huskers Red' 146
Peony 112
Perennial phlox 134
Perovskia abrotanoides 142
Persicaria amplexicaule 'Alba' 142
Pheasant's tail grass 146, 186
Philadelphus 'Belle Etoile' 134
Philadelphus 'Dame Blanche' 128
Phlox-paniculata-hybrids 134
Phyllostachys 46, 50, 86, 100, 172, 192
Phyllostachys aurea 46
Phyllostachys aureosulcata 'Spectabilis' 192
Phyllostachys nigra 148
Phyllostachys vivax 'Aureocaulis' 86
Picea omorika 130
Pickerel weed 30, 36
Pine 130, 144
Pinus mugo 64, 100
Pinus mugo var. *mughus* 64
Pinus nigra ssp. *nigra* 146
Pinus sylvestris 146, 154
Pinus sylvestris 'Glauca' 146
Plantain lily 170, 188
Plum 22
Plume poppy 168
Poaceae 128
Polytrichum commune 130
Pondweed 36
Pontederia 36

Pontederia cordata var. *lanceolata* 30
Poppy 134
Populus nigra 'Italica' 88
Potamogeton 36
Prairie mallow 134
Prairie tickseed 200
Procumbent pearlwort 106
Prunus serrulata 96, 146
Prunus serrulata 'Kanzan' 146
Pyramidal hornbeam 38, 60, 160
Pyrus salicifolia 'Pendula' 142

Q
Quercus ilex 104
Quince 200

R
Red beard tongue 134
Red bistort 142
Red scabious 90, 200
Red trefoil 90
Reindeer moss 106
Rhododendron 58, 146, 158
Rhododendron 'Cunningham's White' 158
Rhus typhina 200
Robinia 18
Robinia pseudoacacia 'Umbraculifera' 160
Rodgersia 72
Rodgersia podophylla 'Rotlaub' 72
Rosa 'Louise Odier' 90
Rosa alba 'Mme Plantier' 140
Rosa 'Mme Isaac Pereire' 90
Rosa pimpinellifolia 104

Rosa rugosa 104
Rose 28, 36, 46, 90, 108
Rose 'Roseraie de l'Hay' 108
Rudbeckia deamii 200
Rudbeckia fulgida 'Goldsturm' 12
Rush 84
Russian sage 142
Ruta graveolens 'Jackpot Blue' 200

S
Sage 26, 38, 134
Sagebrush 104
Sagina procumbens 106
Sagittaria 36
Salad burnet 48
Salix viminalis 162
Salvia 8, 38, 154
Salvia 'Blauhügel' 184
Salvia 'May Night' 108
Salvia nemorosa 'Caradonna' 154, 186
Salvia nemorosa 'Mainacht' 186
Salvia nemorosa 'Steppentraum' 142
Salvia officinalis 'Purpurascens' 38
Sanguisorba tenuifolia 48
Santolina 104, 160, 198
Santolina chamaecyparissus 160, 198
Sacococca hookeriana var. *humilis* 60
Sasa pumila 192
Scented pelargonium 134
Scotch briar 104
Scouring rush 86
Sea buckthorn 104
Sedum 46, 104, 128

Index

Sesleria caerulea 90

Shasta daisy 44, 134, 200

Shrub rose 'Schneewittchen' 158

Siberian flag iris 130

Siberian iris 178

Sidalcea 'Elsie Heugh' 134

Silver grass 128, 140

Silver hedge-nettle 152

Silver tansy 200

Snakeweed 90

Snowball tree 130

Snowdrop 28

Snowy woodrush 88

Soleirolia soleirolii 108

South American vervain 26, 44, 134, 142, 162

Spiny bear's breech 186

Spruce 130

Stachys 152

Staghorn sumach 200

Stipa 26, 90, 108, 136, 146, 154, 168, 178, 186, 200

Stipa arundinacea 146, 186

Stipa gigantea 90, 136, 154, 178

Stipa tenacissima 200

Stipa tenuissima 26, 108, 168

Stonecrop 46, 104, 128

Straw flower 104

Swedish Highland pine 154

Sweetgum tree 180

Sweet william 134

Swiss mountain pines 64

Switchgrass 142

Syringa vulgaris 'Andenken an Ludwig Späth' 134

T

Tall coreopsis 200

Tall mullein 152

Tanacetum niveum 'Jackpot' 200

Taxus 26, 44, 50, 54, 74, 114, 120

Taxus baccata 50, 74, 114, 120

Taxus baccata 'Fastigiata' 120

Taxus baccata 'Overeynderi' 120

Teasel 134

Tender fountain grass 128

Teucrium × *lucydris* 198

Thalictrum ssp. *flavum* 140

Thuja 144

Thuja occidentalis 'Smaragd' 16

Thuja plicata 12

Thunberg's barberry 188

Tickseed 128

Tilia 82

Tobacco plant 172

Trachycarpus fortunei 86

Tree fern 164

Tree of heaven 54

Trifolium rubens 90

Trumpet lily 72, 112

Tsuga canadensis 146

Tufted hair grass 26, 90, 136

Tufted sedge 86, 112

Tulip 22, 28, 114, 140, 148, 160 180

Tulip 'Black Hero' 148

Tulip 'Prinses Irene' 160

Tulip 'Queen of the Night' 148

Typha 36

Typha laxmannii 84

U

Umbrella bamboo 128

Umbrella grass 30

V

Verbascum 'Cotswold Queen' 152

Verbascum 'Gainsborough' 152

Verbena bonariensis 26, 44, 134, 142, 162

Veronica longifolia 'Blue Giantess' 184

Veronicastrum 142, 172

Veronicastrum virginicum 'Fascination' 142

Veronicastrum virginicum 'Lavendelturm' 142

Viburnum 112

Viburnum opulus 'Roseum' 130

Viburnum rhytidophyllum 146

Viburnum tinus 104

Viburnum × *carlcephalum* 134

Vine 10, 30

Virgin's bower 148

Vitis viniferea 30

W

Wallflower 134

Water plantain 30

Weeping beech 188

Wild sage 186

Wild strawberry 130

Willow 162

Willow-pear 142

Wisteria 22, 74, 100, 112

Woodland sage 186

Wormwood 94, 152

Y

Yarrow 26

Yellow meadow rue 140

Yew 26, 44, 50, 54, 58, 74, 108, 114, 120, 132, 144

Yucca 86, 100, 112

Yucca gloriosa 112

Yucca rostrata 86, 100

Z

Zantedeschia aethiopica 72, 112

Zantedeschia aethiopica 'Crowborough' 72

Zebra grass 16

Dear Reader

You will have noticed that I have taken many of the photographs in this book at garden shows. The reason is that so many of these shows, particularly the Chelsea Flower Show, provide an important platform for garden designers to present their latest work to the public. At this point I would like to thank Lynn Bedoe, Hayley Monckton and the RHS Press Team in London, and also Nancy Collantine, Laura Sullivan, and the team at Fido PR in Manchester for their invaluable assistance to us garden photographers during the very hectic show periods. Naturally, I would also like to thank the garden designers with whom I have had the pleasure to work over the years. Whether they are already world famous or just starting out, their ideas inspire me time after time. Finally, a big thank you goes to my author and friend of over 30 years, Ulrich Timm, whose many publications have reawakened interest in gardens and gardening in Germany.

Gary Rogers

Hamburg, September 15, 2007

Acknowledgements

The author, photographer and publisher would like to thank the owners of the gardens, the garden designers, the landscape architects, artists and landscape contractors for their support and cooperation, which has contributed greatly to the success of this book. Special thanks are due to the Royal Horticultural Society in London, whose three annual exhibitions provide many garden designers with a platform to display their skills and introduce new trends: the Chelsea Flower Show, the Hampton Court Palace Flower Show and the RHS Show at Tatton Park. Thanks are also due to the annual garden events in Germany: the Ippenburger Gardenfestival and the Park & Garden Country Fair in Stocksee.

For their tireless efforts in ensuring an outstanding level of quality, we would like to thank Johanna Hänichen, Ilona Schyma, Vanessa Peters, Justyna Krzyzanowska, Claudia Wester, Viola Egan and Claudia Wilke. Special thanks also go to Siegfried Huck and his team at Wesel Kommunikation Baden-Baden for their exceptional efforts and Klaus Fischer and his team at VVA Kommunikation Düsseldorf for their technical support and patience in pursuit of an exceptional printing result. We would also like to thank Christian Albrecht of Serum Network, Munich, for his highly appreciated expert support regarding the special printing method used.

Original edition Becker Joest Volk Verlag
1st revised reprint March 2009

ISBN 978-3-938100-42-4

Text Ulrich Timm

Photos Gary Rogers

Photo on page 25 Marion Nickig | *page 37* Ferdinand Graf Luckner | *page 55* Friedhelm Hellenkamp | *page 57* Ute Wittich | *page 59* Ralf Joest | *pages 85 and 121* Hans Fahrion | *page 143* Petra Pelz

Typographic design according to the concept by
Karin Girlatschek, Hamburg, Germany

Translation Joanna Saunders

English proof read by James Simmonds

Layout, type matter, picture processing, lithography, and editorial work
MAKRO CHROMA Joest & Volk OHG, Werbeagentur, Hilden, Germany

Printed by Wesel Kommunikation Baden-Baden,
VVA Kommunikation Düsseldorf

Hilden, December 29, 2008